MW01070325

"Our deepest despair usually comes from feeling isolated and hopelessly lost. Luke's riveting story of change is proof that God has a plan for all of us."

—Stan Thomas, Friend

†

"Luke Chance personally understands how the Gospel of Jesus Christ can radically transform a life. The death, burial, and resurrection of Jesus Christ has changed Luke from his selfish and shameful past and given him a passion to see many others respond to God's gift of life. Luke's story continues to remind us that no one has gone beyond the limits of what God is willing and able to forgive."

—Jake Schwartz, Lead pastor of church in community

†

Anyone who has ever felt the power of redemption will relate to this story. Still, I'm not sure in all my life that I have ever seen or witnessed the power God turn one huge mistake into something so glorifying to His kingdom. I want to make it very clear, as I have to Luke in the past, that I do not condone what he did, but I recognize sin is sin, and I will not cast the first stone. At the end of our earthly time, it is up to our Heavenly Father to decide who enters the kingdom of heaven for all eternity, not me. I choose forgiveness and believe in the power of second chances, the same way that I have been extended grace and mercy for my sins.

I knew Luke from high school basketball. I knew Luke as the guy who could consistently make half-court shots and banked-in baseline threes. I knew Luke as the first guy to visit me in the hospital after my heart surgery, and I knew Luke as the guy who would invite me to his house and grill out for me. I knew Luke as the funny guy who would constantly extend a helping hand or give you the shirt off his back. I knew Luke as the teacher who made kids laugh but always got through to them with his unique teaching style. I knew Luke in many different lights growing up and even post-college, but I did not know Luke as a Christian. So do I think that what Luke did and all he has gone through is a unique way to lead him to the Lord? Yeah, big time.

I've never once doubted that God works in mysterious ways. As stated earlier, I knew Luke as everything other than a Christian before prison, and eight years later, I know him as a redeemed son of God. Luke is a man with a heart on fire, leading more people to the Lord and watching Jesus save more lives for eternity than probably several pastors in this world. This book is not a story about a felon. This story is a redeeming one about a man of God who committed a felony. Luke would be the first to tell you that what he did was wrong and that he was completely at fault. If you can let your guard down for even a second, you will see the power of grace and mercy that our Lord demonstrates to *all* of us, no matter how small or large the sin we commit. Praise Jesus for this kind of love. Thank you, Father, for all the second chances in life. We do not deserve them, and we'll never be able to repay You, so we thank You for the cross, and we thank You for giving Luke the courage to step out of darkness and into Your light.

—Ben Wilson, Friend

†

By reading Luke's story, we can see that God's purpose for our lives is something that unfolds in large and small ways, all for God's greater purpose. Knowing Luke and being with him through parts of his journey allows me to ask myself, "Am I allowing God to use me for His purpose, or am I using God for mine?"

I encourage you to ask the same thing of yourself. I realize that often the slightest circumstances change the direction of our lives. How could I have known that the stranger who offered me a Diet Coke would become a mentor, encourager, and best friend; one who, after all these years, continues to help guide not just me, but also others, with his knowledge, character, encouragement, and faith in God? Thank you, Luke, for being you.

—Sammy Lucas, Friend

†

# GOD DOESN'T WASTE A THING

MEETING CHRIST BEHIND BARS

## LUKE CHANCE

WESTBOW
PRESS®
A DIVISION OF THOMAS NELSON
& ZONDERVAN

WestBow Press books may be ordered through booksellers or by contacting:

WestBow Press
A Division of Thomas Nelson & Zondervan
1663 Liberty Drive
Bloomington, IN 47403
www.westbowpress.com
844-714-3454

ISBN: 978-1-6642-8737-2 (sc)
ISBN: 978-1-6642-8738-9 (hc)
ISBN: 978-1-6642-8736-5 (e)

Library of Congress Control Number: 2022923622

Print information available on the last page.

WestBow Press rev. date: 01/11/2023

# FOREWORD

The definition for relentless is oppressively constant or incessant. In my time knowing, relating, and observing Luke's life, the word relentless comes to mind. It's how he lives. It's how he relates with people. Most importantly, it's how he pursues Christ. God has shown up in a staggering number of times in his life, and this book tells the story of only a few of them. What I've told Luke on many occasions is that God is jealous and possessive of getting glory. So as Luke, and all of us, walked in obedience to His will, God was in his story. Was it always visible or evident? No. Was it always comfortable? Certainly not. Was it always what Luke thought God would want? Absolutely not! That will all become evident to you in the pages to come. So why was it not some of those things listed above? Because God. Because God wants the glory. Because as Luke would eventually look back on his journey, all he could say is God. As it says in Ephesians 1:4, before God made the dirt Luke walks on, He chose him, loved him, and it pleased Him! That is what I see all throughout this story. Before Luke knew God, God was working, orchestrating, and drawing Luke to himself. So, friends, as you read this testimony, know this: God is in your present. He is in your situation. He may or may not deliver you from present pain or harm, but you can know that God is there in the "during." He's working, orchestrating, and drawing you and me to Himself for His honor, for His glory.

Be blessed!

Chaplain Trent Seton

# PROLOGUE

Scared and ashamed, questioning if life was even worth living anymore, Luke made a decision. Luke left his office, went home, picked up a knife and a bottle of pills, and headed out of the door. Realizing that he couldn't bring himself to use the knife to do this, he threw it out the car window. Scared that the pills wouldn't finish the job, those also went out the window. He went to Walmart to buy a black sweatshirt and headed off to a local railroad crossing. As he walked over the multiple tracks, he felt each one with his hand to see which track was vibrating from a coming train. Pulling the hood of the sweatshirt tight about his face, to blend in with the darkness of night, he lay down with his head on the track. As the noise of the coming train got louder and louder, he curled up in the fetal position and closed his eyes tight, knowing this was the end. Somehow, as the train came rushing past, it ended up on the track behind him. Slowly standing up, bewildered, and trying to figure out what had just happened, he headed home toward a twenty-year prison sentence, a sentence where our paths would cross in 2014 and redemption would begin in the name of Jesus.

Chaplain Craig Ryan

Image by Tony Mann

CHAPTER

1

I am thirty-one years old, sitting alone in a seven-foot-by-ten-foot cell completely built of cinder blocks that were painted the most depressing color of green—one that can best be compared to pea soup. In the middle of the cell is my combination steel toilet and sink, the same one that just six hours prior I was washing away my tears in, trying to calm myself down. As I sit on my steel bunk bolted into the cinder blocks, I struggle to look at the door. The same prison door that slams shut to remind me of my new home for the next twenty years is now the door that swings open as three members of a predominately white gang run in with prison shanks in their hands. This same door that is supposed to be opened by only me or an officer to keep me safe has now been opened by an officer to facilitate the threatening of my life.

Since the gavel struck down that morning before Thanksgiving in 2013, I have had many out-of-body experiences from my normal "white-collar" lifestyle as an educator and coach in the California suburbs, but this one was unique. This experience was different; it rocked me to my core and left me in a sense of panic and depression I never thought possible. I am staring blankly into a mirror that is also made of steel and bolted to the walls as well, and all I can think is I am not even one year into a twenty-year sentence and, as far as I am concerned, would be better off dead than a moving target for the gangs to attack. I'm full of confusion, anger, and anxiety, and I cannot blame anyone but myself for my situation. At this point of my life, I know about the word *God*, but I do not know the Word *of* God. I most certainly do not have a relationship with God, nor do I know the truth of who He is or what He can do. I also do not believe He can do something positive with this mess I have created. It is at this point, in this very dark and cold cell, that I am about to get a kick start into a very true realization I don't even come to recognize or understand for another three years, and that is *God doesn't waste a thing!*

Let me begin by very clearly stating I do not want to spend one more night in prison; however, I can also make the bold statement that I am thankful for every moment I have to spend locked up. It goes without saying I was sad for moments of this time. I was scared for seasons of this journey, and it was not at all smooth sailing the entire time. I am not saying I was thankful during those times. I'm saying now I was thankful during those times. I am saying today I am thankful for what those times taught me, including how they allowed me to grow and how I was able to build my faith in God and His truth and not in my desperation, depression, or circumstance. It is only with God and the work of the Holy Spirit that I can confidently explain God doesn't waste a thing. He never wastes a moment, a death, a prison sentence, a tragedy, or a life-altering day. Nothing at all is wasted. By no stretch of the imagination am I saying what I did, and will share in this book, is anywhere close to as important as what God did. He gets *all* the glory. I will stand firm, though, that God requires us to move like Moses at the Red Sea. God supplies the moments, and often we must reply with the movements.

Prior to me going into prison, I was a spoiled, self-centered, selfish man who had low self-esteem with an imbalanced sense of self-worth. I found my value and identity in not only what others thought of me, but also in many ways those I didn't even know and what they might think of me. I pushed my family away. I always chose my own agenda. I put my wants and needs over my wife's. I chose to ignore her love. I instead chose to view it as an obligation from her. As I write this now, I can see lots of embarrassing and hurtful traits I had. Many of the people in my life were unaware of these traits as I did a fantastic job of hiding them. I refer to this time in my life, as I learned in therapy, as my "pretend normal" phase. This was a time when I was busy coaching and hanging out with my friends, coaches, and team. When people in the community saw me, they would see a confident man who was often the life of the party and the center of attention. I was rarely alone. I would later come to realize it's because when I was alone, I was forced to deal with who I really was and what I was thinking about myself and others. I spent so much time and energy trying to convince those around me I was in control, happy, and healthy that I began to believe my own lies. I began to believe I had no value if I wasn't pleasing others. I felt I was unlovable, and eventually, everyone was going to leave me. It was during this time that I saw the only way to not feel like that was to always be attending places where I felt accepted and loved. I reflected during this time and questioned if I could ever change, and the truth of the matter was I could, but not on my own. Only with the help of Jesus in all areas. I truly had to die to myself so a new, redeemed *me* could be born again.

I went into the Department of Corrections (DOC), not only with all those selfish traits, but also with fear and anxiety about how I would ever survive a day, let alone a twenty-year prison sentence. But it's through the Father's mercy, love, and grace on my life that I can look back and see glimpses of Jesus and how He molded me into the man I am today. Through the truths I will share here in a bit, God crafted me into the best version of me I could be at this time, and He is not finished—and never will be. I am a better son, brother, uncle, friend, and colleague, and if God wills it, someday, again, a better husband. I am not just a Christian; I am also a Christ follower.

The first prison I went to was California City Correctional Facility. California City was a private prison run quite differently than a state prison. The privates are far less security-minded, with far more leniency from staff and less control in movements and monitoring the violence and illegal behaviors. Private prisons often have minimal programs and activities, and this creates more boredom and trouble as men choose to exert their energy in more dangerous and destructive ways. A state facility spends more time and energy monitoring the housing units and is far more cognizant of who they are placing together as cellmates. This was rather apparent, as when I got to California City, I was immediately placed into a four-man room, which is not the norm for most prison cells, especially for a brand new inmate. Within minutes of walking into the cell, I could immediately feel the pressure weighing down on me to find a way to live a lie. It was in the first hour of moving into the room that two things happened. First, I noticed all three of my cellmates had swastikas on their bodies and no hair on their heads. The second was I was asked what my crime was and what my sentence was. I lied to all of them and said I got twenty years, which was about the only thing I said that was true, for selling steroids to families in my community. That lie lasted for about three minutes when they said selling steroids does not carry a twenty-year sentence and that most drug charges do not even come close to that range. I was so new, scared, and inexperienced that I didn't even know what I didn't know.

Over the next day and a half, I went to the library and checked out a couple of books. I sat in the pod and watched the Spanish channel with the Hispanics in the pod. I called home as much as possible, but my parents were in Disneyland with my brother and his family. It was a trip I was supposed to be on, and that was planned back when I was married and before I got in trouble. I'd lie on my bunk with wadded-up toilet paper in my ears, faking to be asleep so I would not have to answer any more questions. As I lay on my bunk, I could hear them discussing how they knew what I did to get sentenced to prison and how they would not allow me to stay in that room with them anymore.

The following morning we got up and went to breakfast. When I came back to the room, I was followed in by the three of them, and they shut the door behind themselves. All of them had on gloves so they didn't get cuts or bruises from a fight, and a couple of them were holding prison shanks in their hands. I was told, at this point, I was a worthless sex offender and that I had the choice between two options: I could check in and get out of the room, or I could fight them all right then and every day following until I either died or decided to check in. I tried to reason with them as I could not figure out how three guys I didn't know would want to not just fight me but also be willing to kill me. I was trying to reason logically in an illogical place. Prison and its politics do not care about logic, and I was getting a crash course in what some of them did care about and how they chose to deal with it. I told them I didn't even know what the term check in meant, so they told me to go out into the pod and hangout and when they announced "count time, lock down" refuse to lock down. I then asked what I was supposed to do with all my stuff, which, two days into prison, were literally just my three pairs of "Blues," which were my state clothes, and two rolls of toilet paper. It wasn't a lot, but when you don't have much, you want to know where what you do have is. They told me not to worry about it, they would throw it in a trash bag and hand it to the cops. With no desire of fighting or getting stabbed and ultimately dying, I chose to go sit in the pod until count time. Count time came, they ordered me to lock down. I told them I could not do that. They asked why, and I told them if I go lockdown, I will be placed in a violent situation. They did not care and just screamed louder as three cops came into the pod and said it was a direct order. Again, I told them I could not do it as every single person in the pod was looking out their cell-door windows and laughing at me. It was after this refusal that I got handcuffed and taken to the sergeant's office. There, I was informed I would be getting a write-up. This would get me more points added to my already-high security status, and I would be sent to a maximum-level facility, where I was certain I would not survive. With no sympathy from the cops, I was sent to the hole to await my write-up hearing and eventually get moved out. Two days later, only fifty hours into my twenty-year sentence, I was shipped out without a write-up.

Let's recap, shall we? In just over two days, I had my life threatened by inmates, been threatened by the cops with a write-up, and basically been told to leave the entire prison yard. Quite the long road to go.

God doesn't waste a thing.

# 2

I can still picture the moment when I was transferred to Mule Creek State Prison (MCSP), which is another private prison. And like California City, even though I was not there long enough to find out, it is not known for having many programs, jobs, rehabilitation, or opportunities. Mule Creek also had a reputation for being more corrupt and violent than a state facility, and here I was, getting dropped off right in the middle of another rough situation. After a quick interview with my case manager, where all she wanted to focus on was how long I was going to be away from family, she informed me I would be a perfect fit for a job in the kitchen, handing out dinner rolls. So that became my job. My new career path was to count to two and give out rolls for every meal. The staff in the kitchen sarcastically told me I was the most qualified for this job since I have a master's degree in education and experience as a math teacher. I stood in that kitchen, one of maybe thirty guys total, with ten of us crammed into a fifteen-foot serving line. I hated how packed that kitchen was. It was cramped, tense, and filled with hatred. I did my best to stack rolls and avoid eye contact. My new goal was to just blend in. This was so out of character for me. But that is what fear and terror will do. It will distort all your natural instincts and personality traits.

This job certainly gave me perspective into my attitude and my pride. Counting to two a few thousand times a day provided me an opportunity to humble myself, listen to authority, and be patient in times of utter frustration and disappointment. To add insight into this five-month span of my life, I had a central goal, a focus if you will, of just trying to get by every moment of every day without being picked on, bullied, hurt, or harassed. Basically, I was trying to go unnoticed. I remember, at this time of my life, I did not know anything about the Bible. I was not even sure if there was a God. To be completely honest, I am not even sure if I knew what there actually was to believe in. Yet through some terrible events, God still worked in my life to bring beauty from the brokenness.

Every night after work, when I would go to take my shower, I would get yelled at. I would walk out of my cell, which was at the top of the stairs on the second tier, and as I made my way down the steps to the main pod floor, which had four old payphones attached to the wall on one side and four showers open to the rest of the pod on the other side, I would get harassed. When I got to the bottom of the stairs, sitting in the corner, all day and all night, were the "White Boys." They would call out names to me based off assumptions they made about my crime. They would shout "SO" or "creep" or many much-worse names. And that is just what they would do on a good day. On a bad day, they would follow me into the shower, threaten me, and try to steal my clothes and towel. These guys do this to intimidate people with a sexual offense. At this point, I felt weak and worthless as I couldn't fight them all. And I am still so new to prison, I have yet to figure out how to even do time. As much as this made me uncomfortable, it doesn't even register when compared to the series of events that are about to play out in my life. One night I was sitting in the cell, watching *The Tonight Show with Jimmy Fallon*, when I changed the channel over to the local news, and I saw my face and my crime being broadcasted. I learned I am going to also be on the front page of the newspaper, and it is evident I have just become the most notorious inmate at this and most other facilities. About five minutes later, my prison door gets popped open, which is not a good thing, as only the guards and myself can open the door, and clearly, it is not me this time. Making matters worse, several of those same gang members entered the room and informed me that they were now aware of my crime, that I am not going to live, and that I need to leave their pod before that happens. While saying this, I'm also shown what my future will be if I don't leave as they flash me their shanks. To the best of my knowledge, these shanks were fashioned from parts of metal ripped off a bunk bed then sharpened, with a homemade handle attached. I was terrified, but I also didn't want to leave another pod out of fear. Thank God for what transpired next. I can say that now, but during the crisis, I did not have a clue of what I was going to do, let alone what God was putting into action. For the next two days, I was informed it wasn't safe for me to work in the kitchen handing out dinner rolls. I was told this by the staff, yet they had no strategy or concern for me to survive the other twenty hours a day I had to spend there.

As I went through the day in the cell house, I was followed 100 percent of the time by two of the recruits in that same gang. These new recruits were known as missiles as the older gang members would send them into a situation to wreak havoc and blow things up. These youngsters would do this with no concern of the consequences as it was how the recruits earned their way up in the gang. They were told to record what I did, when I did it, and where it was done. This creates a rather uncomfortable "fish in a fishbowl" way of living. The guards were told numerous times that I was going to be hurt, and they chose to ignore the warning and stated, "There are plenty of SOs around, it won't be a loss."

[Note: I was made aware of this after speaking to my father and then confirmed four years later, but that is jumping ahead in this book.]

That day, around three in the afternoon, I was sitting in my room when the door flew open, and what must have been about five guards came running in, screaming at me to "get up, turn around, and cuff up." At the time, I could not understand what was happening; I wasn't doing anything wrong. I was the one *being* threatened, and now I am cuffed up and being marched out through the whole pod. With over one hundred sets of eyes all piercing through me, I couldn't help but feel embarrassed and ashamed for my life and my situation. One thing I later learned through my prison time was that things like this become more common, but the reaction it got never did. Men who you thought were your friends would look away while some would yell hateful remarks. Some would stay silent. None, however, ignored the drama and theatrics of the prison show playing out in front of them. I left the pod and was pushed through another door with lots of clamoring and yelling going on from the inmates around me and the officers. During this time, I noticed one of the officers was walking with me and the others were filming this entire event. It was as if I was going to begin fighting back, and that would be the evidence needed to convict that act of stupidity. It turns out that recording an inmate being taken to segregation is a prison norm as being handcuffed is often met with violence. A few more metal doors were opened and shut as the guards pushed me through what was now the empty, narrow, depressing hallways of the cell house as I was being led outside of the unit. Once outside, I heard an officer begin to laugh and say, "This should be funny," as I was paraded along the entire Mule Creek rec yard filled with more than three hundred guys playing softball, working out, and passing their time walking the track.

It is at this 150-yard portion of the walk where I heard the majority of the guys yell threats, call me names, and shout other disgusting things as I passed by. I was led into the main prison building and directed into a room with the plastic name plate on the door that read "PPOU." This was the office of the Private Prison Observation Unit. As I was forcibly pushed into the office, I looked at the man behind the desk. I noticed he looked different from the rest of the workers at Mule Creek. He had a very nice business-style haircut, a suit, and a tie and seemed to have confidence in himself. It was a confidence different from the rest of the officers. It wasn't arrogance. It was assuredness in who he was. This man told the guards to uncuff me and leave the room, which they didn't want to do, so he repeated the order more clearly. When the guards left, he introduced himself to me and informed me I was not in trouble. He told me his name was Paul and asked if I was OK, to which I looked at him and plainly said, "NO!"

He took a second, nodded, and said he was sorry, and then he hit the speaker button on the phone and said, "Jack, I got your son here, and he is safe."

God doesn't waste a thing.

# 3

As I sat there in that office with Paul, I heard my dad speak. "Lukey, are you OK? Your mother and I love you."

I completely lost it. I began to sob uncontrollably. My dad sounded so scared; he hadn't called me Lukey since I was a little kid, and here I was, putting my mom and dad through a living nightmare. Through the tears and him and Paul talking, I began to realize this type of activity is not normal in a prison. Something was happening here that I could not explain. Being able to have the beauty of hindsight now, I can definitively state it was God all along, although in that moment, I just thought it was strange to have my dad on the phone, talking to Paul, who was being so kind and empathetic. That just does not happen in the Department of Corrections. I am so thankful to Paul, for his politeness and his professionalism. Paul chose to have me go to the "hole," administrative segregation or "ad seg," for my protection as he would try to figure out where I could be safe. Protection is a strange word in this scenario. On one hand, I must be isolated in a dark eight-by-five-foot room, twenty-four hours a day, all alone so I can continue to even live to see the next day. Yet at the same time, this isolation eliminated all human interaction and was the beginning of an emotional roller coaster that almost killed me from the inside. So there I sat, waiting for answers, answers that did not come.

Paul did not tell me much more about the situation as he didn't think I could or should try to handle it at the time. A few of the guards were giving me a hard time because of my crime and were finding every excuse to bully me from the inside. The only thing I remember being a positive throughout those seven days in the hole was that Paul brought me two Nelson Mandela books my parents sent in for me to read and a pack of Red Vines. After my week alone, I was shackled up and informed I was going to be moved back to Wasco State Prison (WSP), in Wasco, as they continued to figure out my next stop.

On the journey out of Mule Creek, I was riding in the back of a van with six other prisoners being moved for one reason or another. About a half hour into this ride, a couple of the guys in the very back were joking about how great it would be if the van got into a wreck, rolled, and they would be able to jump out and make a run for it. Maybe it was just me, but I thought this comment was odd. Either way, I couldn't help but think about how out of place I felt. While these guys were planning an escape via an accident, I was trying to plan out how I would stay near the van to prove I was not trying to escape. Here I was, with more than nineteen years left to serve, and I was afraid to run because I didn't want to get more time. Yet the guys behind me had less than five years left. I didn't have much to say that ride, nor did I want to draw any attention to myself, as I was not sure if they saw me on the news or walking through the yard in handcuffs. All I can really be sure of was I was leaving another prison, and it was not on good or safe terms. In eight months, I had managed to go from San Bernardino County Jail to WSP. From there, I went to Cell House 5, which is the transfer unit at San Quentin State Prison in San Quentin, until I went to California City for three days. I then get shipped back to Cell House 5 for a few days as they waited to move me to WSP again for about a four-day layover. I leave WSP that time to head to Mule Creek, which I am now leaving after a little over a half a year to go back to WSP yet again. How was I ever going to survive the next two decades?

Would I ever feel safe again? At this point, I'm not sure what that word even means anymore. Would I be able to make my way through a day feeling comfortable? The thought of ever being able to better my situation seemed so impossible that I couldn't even close my eyes at night as dreams were replaced with nightmares: the sound of the door being popped open, the picture of grown men running into my cell with homemade shanks in their hands and hate in their eyes and hearts and no reason for either; the feeling of the metal on my wrists and ankles, the words of the officers screaming at me as I get shoved through an entire facility, being put on display for all to laugh at.

Once again, WSP is my current residence. However, this time I am not allowed to be out of my cell with anyone else, let alone be able to use the phone, go to the chow hall, or even shower regularly. I am in protective custody. I am on twenty-three-hour-a-day lockdown, and I'm given the choice once a day to use the phone for twenty minutes; go outside, which consisted of standing in a ten-foot-by-six-foot cage surrounded by a thirty-foot brick wall; or the last choice, to take a shower. This type of incarceration is known as twenty-three and one, and there are a fair number of men who are imprisoned at the California State Prison - Centinela who must deal with this for years because they are the highest level of security threat. Yet here I sit in the same situation. Day after day, when I was asked to make my decision, I would choose the phone so I could try to reach my parents. Often, when I tried to call, they were not around their phones as the time the guards gave me the phone was never a consistent hour of the day. When I did finally get a hold of them, most of the time was spent with them trying to calm me down and telling me I was going to be OK. I had a real difficult time understanding how that could be, let alone believe it could be true.

After weeks of this, I began to lose track of time and what day of the week it even was, and to be honest, it was irrelevant as my life was not one of significance or scheduling. I was making choices that were not healthy, and it was taking a toll on my body. My dad finally convinced me, after weeks of ignoring my hygiene, to choose to go shower instead of asking for the phone. I was then introduced to what the men inside of solitary confinement must deal with each time they get to go shower. Two officers came to the cell door and told me to get into my underwear and to turn around and walk backward to the still shut and locked cell door. I got to the door, and they opened the slot in the door where they slide the food into the cell for meals. They had me squat down, put my hands together and place them behind me and through the slot. They then handcuffed me and had me walk back into the center of my cell, where they then opened the door and took me by both arms and walked me to the shower. This is a two-foot-by-three-foot room made completely of metal on three sides but open bars on the side facing the day hall so they could always see me for security reasons. After being uncuffed the same way I was cuffed at the start, I was told to get naked and that the shower would begin in a bit. The shower began, and roughly seven minutes later, the water stopped, shampoo still in hair and soap on body, and I was left to stand naked in the shower for the remainder of the hour. This moment was one of sadness and nerves. I felt so bad for myself and for those who deal with this every day of their sentence. As I stood there, I began to cry as I realized that of all the feelings I was overwhelmed with at this time, one thing I did not feel was the feeling of being human.

I get back from the shower, and I am immediately reminded of my new community. Living right next to me is a guy who every day would defecate in the middle of his floor and then spread it all over the walls and door of his cell. He would yell at the top of his lungs that someone is attempting to get into his room and kill him. The guards would spend their energy banging on his door and screaming back for him to knock it off. They would ask why he was doing this; the only reply they would be given was the feces on the walls and doorway was the only thing that could repel the "killers" from entering the room. I did not know it at the time, but this is some real spiritual warfare type of activity. Knowing now what I do about that type of warfare, it aligns completely with the agenda of the devil, which is to steal, kill, and destroy. Wish I would have had the faith and experience to fight in this battle, but I had no clue what to do. All I could do was try my best not to get sick from this excruciating and disgusting smell, one I had never experienced in my life before or after this moment, as he and I shared an air vent, which did not help matters at all.

God doesn't waste a thing.

# 4

I tell these stories not to gain sympathy but rather to create a perspective and insight into what I am beginning to picture the next nineteen years of my life being like for me. I am thinking that it is going to be filled with: no hope, no joy, and no love, with an abundance of gut-wrenching moments of stench and shame. Throughout this time at WSP, I'm trying my best to keep it together, and I think I am doing a good job, that is until I get a visit from my mom and dad one morning. I get awoken the day of the visit to my eyes watering and a devastating cough I cannot get rid of. I press my face up to the sliver of a window in the door and have just enough of an angle to see the Special Response Team (SRT) bulldozing their way into a room to remove an inmate. This, of course, is happening after they have already dispensed pepper spray, not just in his door, but also in our entire hallway.

A few hours later, I'm told to come out of my room and to get ready for my visit. I wonder, how do I really get ready to see my mom and dad in these current circumstances? No change of clothes, no consistent showering, no deodorant, and a beard that has not been groomed or trimmed for three months. Since I'm an offender who is living in the twenty-three and one section of the prison, I am informed, if someone from the general population gets a visit, I will have to end mine. When I arrive at the visitation room and I get the handcuffs off, I am reminded to keep my hands on the table the whole time. I am let through a last set of sliding doors, where I see my mom and dad at the table. I notice immediately my mom has tears in her eyes while my dad is doing his best to be strong. I walk in and give them the allotted three-second hug and sit down across them with shame, sadness, and desperation. I have my head down as I grab their hands, and all I can think of is how much of a disappointment and failure I am as a son to these amazing parents. I hate that I have forced this situation into their life. I remember telling my parents and myself hundreds, if not thousands, of times there is just no way this is going to get any better. With their hands around mine, I look up and begin to cry as I ask them what I should do or, better yet, what I could do. My dad informed me he had been in contact with the Department of Corrections Headquarters and spoke to them about placing me into permanent protective custody (PC). I asked what that would entail, and he told me I would be moved to Kern Valley facility in Kern, California, where I would serve my time without programs, little to no rec time, and very few opportunities to do anything productive other than sit in a pod and feel "safe."

During this conversation, my dad repeatedly pulled my hands down to the table as I was constantly rubbing my forehead raw. This must have been a side effect of the three months of lockdown with no human contact. This raised the level of urgency in my parents' eyes as they could see I was mentally deteriorating. By the end of the visit, it was decided we would try to get placed into PC. We would do what we could to go spend the next nineteen years in a pod doing little but staying alive. To thrive was not an objective anymore. Instead, the priority became to survive until the year 2032.

My family reached out once again to DOC HQ and was insistent that I get moved to PC as soon as possible. This request was met with the comment that I must request this process myself, which, at the time, was annoying, but I see how it makes sense now. I reached out to learn about the process. I was told the first thing I needed to do was send a note, which, in prison, is known as a "kite," to a case manager I have never met and ask to begin a process I know little about but will alter the next two decades of my life. I got the information, I asked for the kite, and I sent the note. At which point, I am reminded by the guards that things do not go quick in DOC, so I should get comfortable waiting for some time longer. A couple of weeks later, I got word back that I have been scheduled to interview with the protective custody board to allow them to ask questions of me to help them make their decision on my future housing situation.

It is important to mention that, at this time, I am aware of God, but I still do not know Him intimately, I have not given my life to the Lord, and I certainly did not trust and believe He is doing things to benefit my future. I did not know yet what I needed to about faith. Plainly said, I would pray by rattling off my list of wants to Him and tell Him what is best for my future, which, at this time, is to go to Kern Valley. I am sitting in prison because of how great of choices I make, yet I still believe wholeheartedly I am the one who knows what is best, and this is my mindset going into this interview. This was a chance for God to show me that He is there and that He listens to me by getting me safely into protective custody.

# 5

After another month goes by, it has been roughly five to six months of living in twenty-three and one solitary confinement. I am beyond ready to get this process underway of getting out of WSP and head toward Kern Valley. I am taken to the interview, which is done over videoconferencing, and I am sat down with the guard who escorted me into the meeting and a man I have never met. I learn he is my case manager, and he is there to speak on my best interests. Well, he didn't say one word other than to verify, when asked in the meeting, that I am California inmate no. 136726. The meeting began with the lady on the screen who oversaw the PC board and hearing. She informed me she had allotted ten minutes for the meeting, which seemed odd as it was, in my opinion, what was going to decide if I live or die. She then asks me my name, and I tell her, but she does not believe me. She then asked the case manager, and this was when he confirmed my identity, and she replied, "Wow, you don't look anything like your prison profile picture. That's great, you created a disguise for yourself with your beard."

I cannot believe it; she thinks I've grown out this giant beard to not only disguise myself, but also that I will keep it for the next nineteen years. I anxiously interrupt her and inform her I am not keeping this beard, and the only reason I have it is that I am not allowed a razor in the hole for security reasons, and this beard is getting trimmed as soon as possible. It completely blows my mind that her best plan for me to survive is to grow out a beard, completely ignoring the fact that all my clothes have my name and number on it, thus making a disguise is not just ridiculous, but also impossible. This meeting is not going well in my opinion, and it only gets worse when she tells me that with my education, along with the disguise, she feels I would be successful at another prison. I was not allowed to say anything else, and after seven minutes, I was told the meeting was over and that I would be made aware of their decision soon.

The walk back took about ten minutes, and the whole time I was saying to myself that there is no way I don't get accepted into PC. I cannot comprehend how anybody could look at how I had to leave the last two prisons and think because I am good at math and have a Duck Dynasty "starter beard" that things will be different if I got to general population at another prison. There is just no way. I get walked to my door, raise my left leg then my right leg as they remove the shackles, and I step into my cell to think about my future while lying on my cement bunk. Forty-five minutes later, under the door slides a single sheet of paper.

DENIED.

I reread that word for about fifteen minutes as "DENIED" is stamped on the protective custody hearing form, and I am told shortly after that I will be moving to general population at another facility in the next day or two. It's at this point when tears begin falling from my eyes as I not only tell God how wrong this decision is, but I also try to demand that the guards fix this. Now I am not sure how God reacted to my comments and complaining, but the guards told me in not-so-kind words to "shut up" and that they not only don't have the power to "fix" this, but that they also don't care either. By the end of the week, I am woken up, told to pack my things and get ready to leave. I am then shackled and put on a bus headed toward the state prison located in San Quentin (SQSP).

God doesn't waste a thing.

# 6

I remember arriving at SQSP on August 8, 2014, which was about
six months from the first time I was there. For me to say it was
intimidating at first sight is a massive understatement. It is surrounded
by a giant rock wall, which is not only created using rocks from the
mountain it is built into, but it was also built by the hands of the prisoners
themselves. Think about that: There were men who literally built their
own separation from society, stone by stone, foot by foot. Walking into
Cell House 5 again, knowing this would become my permanent facility,
was scary. I could feel my heart pounding through my neck. Inside was a
level of loud I have never experienced. Two hundred men were screaming
at one another, yelling at the guards, and banging on the bars. It was the
most debilitating noise, and I was about to call this home.

The bars in this place are all painted the most horrific pastel colors.
If I am doing my best to describe the scenery, it looks just like Easter
from 1918, with yellow, purple, pink, and baby blue cells. After a few
nights of this place, a couple of fights, and one suicide attempt by the guy
across the tier from me, I was told I would be moving behind the walls in
thirty minutes. Going behind the walls is what they called moving into
the "big" part of the prison, where this becomes a home rather than a pit

stop. I put my shower shoes, my half roll of toilet paper, and my pad of writing paper into a trash bag as this was all the property I was allowed to have while in Cell House 5, and I headed toward the backdoor, which would open and reveal the inside of San Quentin. It's weird to describe the scenery as awesome, but it really was in an "old-historic" type of way. Most of the buildings were built out of the same stone, in some capacity, that the wall was made from. There was actual grass scattered throughout the compound, which I had not seen since being incarcerated. There was even a river that ran in and out of the prison, going through the walls, which is how the city got water from the Kern River to the eastern part of the town. Even though the scenery was pleasant, it was still scenery from inside of a prison. My nerves were frazzled as I attempted to move into yet another facility, when less than a week ago, I was begging to be placed into protective custody.

God doesn't waste a thing.

# 7

I get processed through property and taken to Cell House 1 to put my stuff into my cell. While getting settled into my cell, I got an uneasy feeling when a couple of the guys in my pod came by to check me out. This is common prison behavior when someone new comes into the pod. It is also unnerving because the guys looked like the men who have caused the dangerous situations in the other two facilities. When I say they looked similar, I am saying both men were bald, covered in tattoos, not smiling, and looked upset that I just entered their world.

A standard process for a new arrival to any DOC facility is to get placed in the kitchen to work for a minimum of sixty to ninety days. I was not thrilled about this prospect, and yet a week had come and gone, and the kitchen never hired me. Instead, I got a kite in the mail saying the GED teacher at the facility needed an assistant with a focus on math, and I was told I was going to be her assistant. The next day, I am at the front of a room with a whiteboard, a marker, and seven "students" working toward their GED.

I have stood in front of thousands of students, taught hundreds of different classes, and have over ten thousand hours of teaching experience, and there was never a day of teaching I ever felt as nervous as I did the first couple of weeks of teaching at SQSP. I kept telling myself I can't let them find out about my past because as soon as they do, they won't listen to me, and they would probably bully me and hurt me. This fear was constantly running through my mind, on repeat, and even though I struggled with these thoughts, I still poured my whole heart and effort into teaching these guys and helping them reach their goals. It was exciting to see a few of them begin to shine. One man in particular, Nash, was granted parole upon the completion of him getting his GED. After a couple of months of him and I studying diligently, and with the help of the guards who let us into the classroom during off times to use the whiteboards, he passed the test and earned his GED along with his freedom.

Nash passing and leaving was amazing, but it was not unique as two others got the same opportunity once they began working with me. This was great because never has the level of my teaching and support had such a huge impact in the lives of my students. This sharing of math knowledge allowed men to go free and families to unite. Kids got their fathers back, wives got their husbands back, and parents got their sons back, and it was not a coincidence. God was right in the middle the whole time. He was showing me He cared about me and the small things as He was revealing Himself to me each day. I just couldn't see it for myself yet! Looking back now, it is amazing seeing how all the pieces began to fall into place for me to later encounter the man who would become not just a mentor, but also a true inspiration in faith.

# 8

One day I wandered down to the prison chapel. I wasn't sure what I was hoping to accomplish once I got there; I just knew I needed to go there. It was that day that I met Chaplain Ty, who took about thirty minutes and listened to me complain and explain my frustrations with my situation and what I was going through. I remember telling Ty God was not present in my situation and that He did not care one bit about me and my future. This inspired Ty to open his Bible to Job and walk me through the sections where Job was doing lots of complaining of his own. After I felt validated and like I was correct, Ty moved us into chapter 38, where God began to question Job. This part of the conversation was not as much fun for me. Our meeting ended with Ty suggesting I meet Chaplain Craig and said he would be a much better person for me to chat with. I told him I would love to do that, and he said he would make sure Craig comes and finds me the next time he gets a chance. I am truly thankful for Chaplain Ty. I am also honored he took the time to speak to me and be my first interaction with the church at SQSP, but I am even more thankful he told me about Chaplain Craig as I began to keep my eyes open for this man.

Getting in to see Craig was difficult because the hours I taught GED were the same hours he worked down in the chapel, and I did not have enough experience in the facility to ask for "days off" or favors. One day I'm in the education building teaching, when I look out the window and I see this man with khakis and a black leather jacket on walking around. I know this is not a guard as he is clearly not dressed like an inmate. In my gut, I felt the urge to go chat with him. I asked my boss if I could step out for a bit, and she said of course, and twenty seconds later, I am shaking hands with the man who will have had the greatest impact on my life, other than my father, on this earth.

Craig Ryan took the time to stop for me, to listen to me, and to care about me. After a quick chat with my boss, Craig informed me he had arranged for me to come to the chapel every Wednesday after the noon lockdown. These were times when he and I would sit and go over anything on my mind. If he only knew what he was getting himself into with that offer. I would show up with my notebook and the Bible he had given me, and I would pepper him with questions for hours on end. Not one time did he ever not answer one of them or tell me to stop. It was in those moments I began to see a man in front of me who lived focused on God and sharing His Word with others. I knew I wanted what he had: an inner peace, a confidence in his identity, and a true love for Jesus.

While sitting in Chap's eight-foot-by-ten-foot office for hours on end, I started to sense a calling to unload a tremendous burden. I didn't quite know what it was, and even worse, I didn't know how to deal with it. Chaplain Craig challenged me to go back to my cell, sit with my feelings, and write down all the guilt, burdens, sins, and secrets I was holding on to. He explained these were areas Satan was using to attack me and keep me from joy and true freedom. The next Wednesday, I walked into his office with my list in hand, and I sat down, and he looked at me and asked if I was ready to experience a breakthrough. Craig pulled a three feet tall wooden Cross off the cabinet in his office and set it down in the middle of the floor between the two of us. He asked me if I was ready to cast my burdens on the One who is capable to carry them for me while freeing me from the guilt. I began to read my list out loud, and Craig helped me take each one of them to God's courtroom and set them at the foot of the Cross. That day, I laid down guilt, lust, past relationships, secrets, ties to the devil, distorted thoughts, anger, and anxiety to name a few. As I sat there in tears, I felt a weight being lifted off my shoulders. Craig led me in a prayer to receive the work Jesus did on the Cross and accept Jesus as my Savior into my heart.

God doesn't waste a thing.

CHAPTER

# 9

I am a Christian! I gave my life to the Lord on January 2015, and I now know that no matter what happens on earth and in my life, I would have an eternal home in heaven. This was and still is the most momentous day of my life, but trust me, life didn't just get instantly easy and magical. It did, however, allow me to look through an eternal lens and change my outlook on life and what is truly important. On January 11, 2015, I got baptized in the San Quentin chapel.

Baptism Reason for Luke Chance
January 11, 2015
@ SQSP with Chaplain Craig

I am choosing to get baptized to show my family, friends, and my Lord Jesus Christ that I outwardly proclaim and passionately accept Jesus Christ into my heart and my life as my savior. I do not expect my walk to become an easy walk from this moment forward, however I can now trust that I will never again be alone on this walk.

God bless you all, thanks for being here for this special occasion in my life!

I love you all,
Luke

I was excited to show those around me that I chose to accept Jesus into my life and that I was committed to walk together with Him. I spent lots of time writing letters to friends on the streets to tell them of my rebirth. Those I was allowed to call, I did so with enthusiasm in my voice and heart. This moment was great as with a smile on my face and joy emanating from my body, I was walking around inside of a prison. I felt true contentedness and could begin to live with hope in my life and, dare I say, future. It reminded me of the time when I was walking the yard, which, again, is prison terminology for the general rec and living area of a facility, at SQSP with a friend of mine, Kyle, who is still a friend of mine to this day. I asked him how he could walk through prison seeming to be so happy, and his answer was heartfelt and simple. He told me he lives each day for Jesus because he has received his freedom by accepting the Holy Spirit in his heart. At the time, that made no sense to me; it seemed ridiculous. Now I have not only experienced it, but I have also felt the change of accepting the Holy Spirit into my life and now walking in that freedom.

A couple of weeks later after my baptism, I was at a 7 Habits of Highly Effective People Graduation in the visitation room. It was one of a few dozen I would attend throughout my time in the Department of Corrections. At this graduation, Chaplain Craig and his clerk at the time, Mark Foster, asked if they could speak to me after the graduation. I was excited anytime I got the chance to speak with Craig, but I was nervous every single time when I spoke to Mark. The reason for this uneasiness was Mark was going into his twenty-fifth year of prison, and much of it was spent in the toughest prisons in California. Mark was intimidating. He was covered with tattoos and had some definite rough edges that had formed through his decades of hard prison time. It was not uncommon to leave a conversation with Mark feeling loved and scared at the same time. Nevertheless, it was another chance to go and meet with Craig.

I get to the chapel for my appointment, and Craig tells me he wants me to sit down and chat with Mark to see how well he and I get along. This is an odd request, but I tried to not question Craig that much. It is essential to the timeline that I make it clear I have discussed openly the details of my crime to Chaplain Craig, yet I have not told any of the inmates at San Quentin about my past. I am honestly just too scared. I am sure others probably knew, I just wasn't going to validate their thoughts by talking about it, and I certainly wasn't going to confirm it for them.

Going into Mark's office for our conversation, I had a plan to deflect and keep it all surface level and not let him get too close. When I walked in, Mark told me to shut the door. After I did that, I sat down, and he said, "So, Luke, what did you do to come to prison?"

Normally, I would have been terrified. However, something was different about this talk with Mark. As I sat there, I felt something inside of me shift; something was pushing me to share my crime with him. Sitting there in the clerk's office, I said to Mark, "Here's what I did to get put in prison."

I informed Mark I was a teacher and a coach, and I got involved in a sexual relationship with a student that led to me getting sentenced to twenty years in DOC. I told him I had to register as a sex offender, and I have been threatened and ran out of two prisons because of this fact. As I sat there with my head down and tears falling from my eyes, I looked up to see Mark staring right at me with tears in his eyes too.

Mark often got described as rude and abrasive from others around the facility, but with me, he was nothing but caring, loving, and forgiving. He and I still had our moments of tension and disagreements, which is common between friends, especially inside of a prison, where you are with that person all day, every day. In the end, though, we always came back to each other as friends and brothers. This brotherhood and support between the two of us was rooted in the love and hope we had in Jesus and His finished work on the Cross.

After I finished chatting and crying with Mark, Chaplain Craig had me sit in the chapel and listen to music until movement. Craig spent the rest of the time talking to Mark. What about, I am not sure, but I had a feeling it was about me and how our conversation went. The next day, Chaplain Craig had me come down to the chapel after I finished teaching GED for that day and asked me if I would like to work for him as the other clerk in the chapel. I would be working with Mark every day and be in the chapel with Craig and the other chaplains to help men who came in to seek counseling. I remember telling Craig I did not feel qualified for this position. He asked me what I meant by that, and I told him I was barely six months into even knowing who Jesus is, and I still have lots of questions myself, not to mention not being able to quote scriptures or even know which Bible story to lead someone who is struggling to. I continued telling him I didn't even know what books are in the Old Testament and which ones are in the New Testament. If I am being completely honest, I had only known that there were an Old Testament and a New Testament for less than a year.

I finished my list of reasons to Craig on why I wouldn't be a good fit by telling him all I was great at is being organized and having the ability to hug and love those who come in the door. Craig said, "Perfect, God will take care of the rest." And just like that, I was hired.

God doesn't waste a thing.

# 10

Normally, when you ask for a job change inside of the DOC, it takes a minimum of three weeks for it to go through, if it happens at all. Well, two days later, I was transferred to Craig in the chapel, which alone is a mighty miracle, one of many that are about to happen in my life. To say this job in the chapel turned out to be a great job would not even come close to being an accurate statement. This job, the moments, and the people I got to share my life with were truly transformative. I earned $0.87 a day, and it was, and still is, the best job I have ever had in my life. I got to spend countless hours with the kindest, most generous people walking on this earth. The volunteers who came into SQSP to share their love of Jesus filled me with joy each time.

A few months into working with Mark, he shared more about his past and how he used to treat people whom he didn't agree with while in prison. He told me all this because he wanted me to see how far God has brought him. Mark's life encouraged me that God can transform lives and hearts if you trust in Him. He also wanted to let me know that he loved me and thought of me as a brother. He confessed to me, the first ten to fifteen years of his sentence, he spent his time doing drugs and selling them to others "inside of the joint." Mark added that it was in those years that he would tell people who had a sex offense that they needed to use the phone and shower while he was at work. He told them, if he saw them out of their cell while he was in the pod, he would make sure they knew that was never to happen again. The way he would teach this lesson was by dragging the men back into their cell and beating them up so badly that they would not ever want to be seen out of their cell when he was around. Mark explained to me, through his testimony, this is another example of the wonder-working power of God and what can happen when God gets a hold of your heart. For years, Mark tried to change his feelings and his behavior but could not get rid of the hate in his heart until God did the work through him.

Mark then dropped his head and asked me if I could do a favor for him. The favor was for me to stand in the gap for the men he bullied, hated, threatened, and hurt over the past twenty-five years (Ezekiel 22:30). I was not sure what this meant, but I told him "yes." Mark then proceeded to apologize to me for all the hate-inspired actions he took and asked for my forgiveness in those situations. This entire time of him confessing specifics to me, eyes filled with tears, allowed him to apologize to the men he hurt and never got the chance to reconcile with. Afterward, Mark and I prayed and asked the Lord to take those feelings of anger and sadness and replace them with joy and love as we took those memories to the Cross and ask Jesus to take them from him. This was such a great moment on many levels as my presence in that chapel allowed Mark to get closure and forgiveness on an issue he had been carrying with him for nearly three decades.

God doesn't waste a thing.

# 11

Being Chaplain Craig's clerk was awesome. It allowed me lots of
opportunities to see God work in many ways. My main job was to
support the chaplains and be encouraging to the men who came
into the chapel that day. I spent countless hours listening to worship music,
studying the Bible, asking Craig and the other chaplains questions. I would
sit with Mark, learning from him and his wealth of knowledge on the Bible
and prison life in general. Mark and I had clerk hours from 7:00 a.m. to
11:00 a.m., noon to 4:00 p.m., and then we would come down to put on
an evening Bible study or worship service from 6:00 p.m. to 9:00 p.m. The
times in between those hours were the prison's mandatory count times. Mark
and I got to the point where we would be in the gym or the yard setting up
services and events during those times as well. The chapel was a safe place.
It was a place where I could learn about myself and help others, all while
feeling closer to the Lord. My time at SQSP began to make sense as did my
life. It was a very odd thing to be locked up in prison, away from my family
and friends, not able to be with my grandmother as she was getting older
and weaker, yet also laughing and feeling helpful and important to others
while working and living in DOC. The more I prayed, obeyed, and trusted
God to lead me, the more favor and blessings I saw show up in my situation.

Prisons are big in many aspects yet small at the same time. You are around the same people all day, every day, and people in prison tend to gossip and talk more than high school girls. This type of chatter is known as "Prison.com" or "Prison Twitter" because it was this constant chatter that spread the information quickly throughout the entire yard and system. I was beginning to be noticed throughout the whole facility as I was in one of the most trusted and visible jobs in the facility. This didn't always sit well with me as in the last two prisons, my outcome wasn't great when people noticed me. My goal was to stay invisible and out of the mix. I mean, it was not even a year ago that I was sitting in WSP, asking to go hide in protective custody, so being invisible and surviving was still my objective. God had a different objective, it would seem. I was now not only working in the chapel and spending what little free time I did have trying to work out, walking with friends, and playing softball with my buddy Stan, but also, I now had a couple of guys asking me if I would be willing to help them with a problem they had.

The men, Kurt and Randy, were friends and had learned that I had a background in education with a master's degree and that I knew how to write and proofread. Both guys had made the choice to take responsibility for their crimes, their pasts, as well as to take ownership of their future. I had the privilege to help Randy write his clemency letter to the governor of California, a letter that would show remorse for his choices that led to him being incarcerated and how he was also committed to making the most out of his future. Randy stated his plans to work in society to help others battling addiction while encouraging them and empowering them to take control of their lives. I can tell you that Randy is out of prison, and he is doing very well. He has created a successful business and helps others reintegrate back into society upon being released from prison.

Kurt was currently taking classes to get his bachelor's degree when he approached me and asked if I would be willing to sit with him and proofread some of his papers. I was a bit apprehensive. Kurt was the strongest guy at San Quentin, with a bench press that was over 415 pounds, not to mention he was in prison for a crime that was committed while he was leading a dangerous gang in California. I prayed about it and felt confident and comfortable that this was a good thing to do and that it would be someone worth investing in. Kurt and I spent countless hours together over the next three years, many of which were spent going through research papers and learning how to dissect information to generate a college-level paper while also explaining how and where punctuation should be added. Kurt was bright and extremely hardworking, and it led to him earning his bachelor's degree. One of the greatest moments I got to experience while at SQSP was being in attendance when the prison held a graduation ceremony for him and allowed his family to attend the event. Since my release, Kurt has continued to thrive inside and has since had another ceremony, this time to commemorate his hard work in completing a master's degree.

It was around this time of helping these men that I began to write to ministries throughout the country, asking for support and if they would be willing to come alongside our chapel and fill some needs we had. I wrote to them that we had roughly nine hundred men who were being housed at SQSP and would love and appreciate any resources they could spare to further God's kingdom in our mission of sharing Jesus throughout these prison walls. I requested books, DVD lessons, faith-based movies, study Bibles, pamphlets, cards for encouragement, as well as loss, all to be sent in to bless the men at SQSP. As an inmate, I was not allowed to write to ministries and solicit donations, so I did all this using Chaplain Craig's name as my contact, with his permission, of course. Shortly after, we began getting replies and boxes sent in, and they didn't stop for a very long time. We got movies and worship albums. We got DVD lessons and cards. We got self-help books rooted in Christ and the power of the Cross, and we got dozens and dozens of study Bibles. This was just the tip of the iceberg in creating more opportunities to share Jesus and love with the men at SQSP and throughout DOC as we were able to share our contacts with other prison chapels. I always loved the movie *Shawshank Redemption*, which is a little weird as I ended up in prison myself, but I have always thought of this time of my incarceration as my Andy Dufresne season. While Andy was in prison, he built and stocked a library for all the men at his facility. This was my goal too. I wanted to create a place where guys could come in and study the Word from a variety of different resources, as well as sit quietly and listen to music or watch a movie with a buddy. Having a place where everyone felt loved, accepted, and safe was of the utmost importance for me, and I am honored to have been a cog in getting this created.

A movie or a CD may have been the reason someone came to the chapel, but it often was not the outcome of that visit. Being in the chapel repeatedly led men to dive into relationship questions and concerns, relationships with themselves, with their families and loved ones, and ultimately with Jesus. It was essential to have them in the chapel, in the "arena" of love and encouragement, so they knew they were safe to explore these areas of their hearts without judgment. It was in these moments when I worked extensively on a term that Doug, a good friend of mine, made up to keep my priorities in place, which was ME 3. What this meant for me was to always put God first, the person who I am interacting with at that time was second, and I was third—ME 3. This meant, when men came down to the chapel with their concerns and issues, they were more of a priority than my own interests. My focus was on showing them agape love, on showing them Jesus, which often ended in prayers and hugs, and more than likely an introduction to Chaplain Craig so they could get his insight on hope and going to the Cross for healing. It was inspiring for me to see so many men take advantage of this safe place, and it was encouraging for me to see a shift in my own entitlement and selfishness as I focused on others for the first time in my life. In that chapel, I had the daily privilege of seeing people learn about God and experience firsthand their faith growing inside of these prison walls. What society and the judicial system had setup to be a dark, depressing, and hopeless place was gone. Instead, we created a warm place where people could find hope and know for a fact that they are loved. And throughout all this time, I have still yet to realize I was asking back in 2014 to go to Kern Valley for PC, and if it wasn't for my beard and being good at math, I would have never gotten to SQSP and this chapel job.

God doesn't waste a thing.

# 12

There must have been twenty to twenty-five different services and studies Mark and I would put on throughout the month. It was a blessing and an honor to spend my time getting to know the men at San Quentin throughout all the different services and seeing where each of their hearts and passions were. Although I didn't practice any other denomination other than Christianity, I still set up and organized the chapel for all the other faiths practiced inside of a facility. On any given day, I would set up services for the Muslims, the Catholics, the Asatrus, the Pagans, the Messianics, a few Hindu guys, and even a service for atheists, if you can imagine that. I took my role seriously as I was the one in position to create a safe, welcoming, and sacred place for the men to worship. Like I stated earlier, I did not believe in what they chose to put their faith in, but I always respected the men themselves, regardless of what they chose to worship. It always upset me when there would be fights in prison over faith because I don't believe that is the way a man of faith should act. I was not the spokesman for Christianity at SQSP. Jesus had that well under control. I was, in many ways, the face and the voice of the chapel, and if I was rude or biased toward a specific denomination, it wasn't going to promote love and unity, which was my goal in the job.

Jesus calls us to love, so I did. I wasn't perfect. I got yelled at lots, but I can confidently say I put God first and tried to be His light every day. This became one of my favorite times of the job, getting to know the hearts and passions of all the different men, staff, and volunteers for their respective groups. It became apparent we are much more alike than different. Yet the world, prison, and life tend to highlight the differences and create hate rather than coming together in love. Hate is from Satan, and once I learned love, real love, beats hate every time, I trusted in the Holy Spirit and led with love.

# 13

I feel it is imperative to highlight what I was going through personally during this season. I was still struggling with fear, a somewhat debilitating fear, the fear of rejection if I disclose to others about my crime. If I dare trust others with my past, will they hate me? Will they threaten me, or as before, will they attempt to kill me? The fear of rejection bled into a fear of my overall safety, which led to a fear of my future and ultimately my life. I wasn't going to trust my life with anybody but myself, even Jesus at this point. Although I had people who knew the details of why I was in prison and still loved me, this wasn't enough to go "all in" and trust. I was maturing in my faith in many areas, but this one—this one right here—I held on to. I was reluctant to lean in and give it to God.

This fear didn't just impact my relationships inside of prison, but I was also nervous about the friends I had on the streets and if they would eventually leave me like so many others had up to this point. I had around a dozen friends, close friends, who all cut ties with me. They ignored my calls and my letters; some even went as far as telling my parents they wanted nothing to do with me or them at this point. This further hurt my feelings and poured fire on the fear of losing others in my life, and since my identity wasn't deeply rooted in Christ at this point, fear ran wild in my life. Because of the actions of some, I let the irrational fear of losing all friends in my life become the narrative I told myself each morning I got up.

What was worse? I had lots of support in and out of prison, more than most, if I am being honest: friends, family, even volunteers and men inside of prison I had met just a year ago, who loved me unconditionally; yet I couldn't focus on the blessings without bringing up the disappointments. This is an unfortunate but common theme that exists in society and prison for sure. We tend to focus on what we don't have instead of appreciating what we do have. I spent a significant amount of my time trying to figure out how to win back those friends who had chosen to walk away. I would walk the yard alone and play out just what I would say to them when/if I get released. This self-talk was not positive, not uplifting, and certainly did not highlight Jesus and his love and work in me. I was hurting and scared, and I thought this would help, but it just made matters worse.

Ben, a particular friend of mine, along with a few others, Nate, Everett, and Max to name a few, have chosen to stay with me throughout all these tough times. I've had the great pleasure of experiencing Ben support and encourage me in a way that has given me the gift of feeling unconditional love and friendship. Ben is a childhood friend of mine and has had his own unique path of walking through trials and struggles yet pushing into Jesus for hope and confidence that God's plan is greater than our circumstances. Ben has dealt with a heart surgery and came through it not only with a healthy heart physically, but also a stronger heart spiritually set on loving others as Jesus loves us. Ben was a friend through my youth and college years. He was involved in my life during my marriage. He was present when I was sentenced and preparing to go to prison. When others chose to run away, Ben made the conscious choice to draw near me and walk with me through this situation I put myself into. How he chose to love me changed my outlook on how someone can live with Christ being the focal point of their life. How Ben reacted when faced with tough situations gave me the encouragement to love others, even when it hurts. There were times when Ben was treated poorly and ignored by some friends for his choice to stand beside me, but he didn't let it affect him. He never chose to respond to unkindness with unkindness. He continued to show them love and grace, even though several chose to unfriend him. He would express to a few of them that he chose to support me, the man, even though he never has, and never will, condone what I did. If that meant he would lose friends of his own, so be it. Ben acted as a Christian does. That is a great perspective, with an identity and self-worth rooted in truth. That is the act of a great friend and an even better man. I have heard it said, "In good times, your friends get to know who you are. In bad times, you get to know who your friends are."

As I have learned, hard times will always reveal true friends. I am eternally grateful for his friendship and his example of how to walk with love.

God doesn't waste a thing.

CHAPTER

# 14

Visits from Mom and Dad were continuing to be great as they would come every third weekend of the month. They chose this schedule to not only get in a family routine, but so they could also say hi to Chaplain Craig as he would walk through visitation on the days he came into prison to preach, which were the third Sundays of the month. This time was special as I got to hug Mom and Dad, and they could see I was doing well. Mom and Dad felt good as I had my job in the chapel, which provided a safe environment with the men I encountered throughout the day. They appreciated this sense of comfort, but they were also aware there never is a guarantee of a safe moment in prison; it can change in the blink of an eye. mark would always tell me, "Luke, prison can get real, real, real quick and that I need to always stay aware of my surroundings." This statement reared its ugly truth more times than I care to count in my seven years of prison living.

One event stands out more than the others while I was at SQSP, and it happened quick. It was a sheets-and-blanket morning, where everyone in the prison is required to turn in their linens to get washed as some men are happy never washing their sheets. It is 5:15 in the morning, and I am sitting in the middle of the pod in Cell House 7, 1-2 left, which is prison speak for Unit 7, left side of the building, floors 1 and 2. I was sitting there, quietly chatting about the day with my friend Stan, and I was telling him I was excited for the service we were putting on that evening. I was always eager for this monthly service as the chapel was always at capacity as the volunteer who came in to preach for this service was previously incarcerated himself, and he had a real gift of connecting his words about Christ to the ears and hearts of the men who attended the service. The man's name was Ramon, and he never missed an opportunity to share Jesus with those of us here at SQSP who chose to come to the chapel.

While sitting there, chatting away, I noticed two cellmates walking in and out of their cell more than normal. To shed some light on the magnitude of this situation, it is essential I paint the picture of the two men involved. One of the guys is a five-foot-ten-inch forty-five-year-old extremely skinny white guy named Squint, who maybe weighs 150 pounds. The other man is Donavan, and he is a rather bulky five-foot-nine-inch thirty-five-year-old black man, who weighs north of 220 pounds. This morning Donavan had his TV on and left the volume up, and Squint could hear it. Now what is customary in prison and in your cell is to plug in headphones so one TV does not disrupt the other. OK, back to the story—Squint went into the room, and since Donavan was not in there, he turned the TV off. That upset Donavan, so he told Squint not to touch his TV, and he turned it back on and once again left the cell. Next thing we know, the TV is off again, and the room is empty. As with most arguments in prison, it stems from a feeling of being disrespected, so Donavan waved for Squint to come back to the cell. Keep in mind, it is not even 5:30 in the morning. As soon as Squint gets to the door, he was grabbed by the neck and shoved into the cell, with the cell door slammed behind. For the next thirty seconds, everyone in the pod was sitting on pins and needles to see what was going to happen. When the door opens, less than a minute later, out walks Donavan, and he just sits down in front of Stan and me. Squint, shortly after, limped out with his hands over his face. These two had just gotten in a fight regarding turning off a TV. It's that quick. It's that small of a thing that can derail not just a day, but also your entire prison future and life.

It would only be a matter of time before it got noticed, and the facility would go on lockdown, and an investigation would ensue. This is, in fact, what happened within the next two hours as a correctional officer saw Squint's face. The loudspeaker goes off over the entire facility, and we are told that we are on lockdown and that all programs and services were cancelled for the day. It is not uncommon to cancel services or programs as DOC puts facility security as its top priority, as they need to investigate the fight and see if it is a singular event or if there is a chance it is the beginning of a racial war inside of the facility. That piece may not have been abnormal, but what happened next is completely abnormal. Nine hours later, as I was sitting in my room, I got a knock on my door from an officer, telling me to go get Mark and go down to the chapel. I jumped off my bunk and headed to the second tier of the pod and gathered Mark, and we went to the chapel and proceeded to set up for the service. Now the service was supposed to be cancelled, but when they called Ramon and told him to turn around because of the fight and lockdown, he didn't. Instead, Ramon kept coming with the intention of sitting in the parking lot to pray over the facility. As he was doing this, a captain walked by his car and noticed him just sitting in a prison parking lot, which is totally abnormal and somewhat alarming behavior for sure, so the captain asked him what he was doing there. After hearing Ramon's explanation, he called back into the facility and got it approved for him to come in since he drove the three hours to get here. Mark and I opened the chapel for the service, completely in shock this has been approved.

Now that is cool and a total God thing to get the service approved in such a manner, but here is where it gets awesome and God-inspired. Since this was the only thing that was going on in the facility this evening—no library, no yard, no rec, just this service—a handful of guys sneaked out of their units just to get out of their cells during the lockdown. Well, God had a different agenda for a few of these men. A couple of those guys settled into the service and sat quietly with eyes full of tears as they ot only heard the message of the Gospel, but also they gave their lives to the Lord that very night when Ramon gave an altar call. These men forever changed the trajectory of their prison path as well as their eternal future. All glory to God. He does not waste a fight. He will not waste a lockdown or even the timing of a captain walking to his car after work.

God doesn't waste a thing.

# 15

One of the most impactful opportunities I had the privilege of being a part of while at San Quentin was introducing an organization called God Behind Bars (GBB). Through the work and collaboration of SQSP and GBB, we were able to bring this program inside the facility, which provided an avenue for the families of the men at SQSP to watch the same church service as their loved ones inside. During this time of my incarceration, I was gaining confidence, not just in how to do prison time, but also in myself. This confidence was a byproduct of drawing closer to Jesus daily. This is a relevant point to make because when this program came to SQSP, it meant I would have a much more visible role in the facility than I already had. It also meant Mark and I would be setting up and running GBB every Saturday for over one hundred men and up to fifteen volunteers. Thinking back to my years as a teacher and coach, this would have not been a problem or even worrisome because I thrived on all that attention. I looked at those times as an opportunity to get everyone's eyes on me. However, a couple of things were different now. One, I was no longer in a safe school, where I knew I was adored; now I was in a prison, where it was likely that numerous people disliked, hated, and probably wanted to kill me. Two, I was going through some personal growth as I have now identified, with the guidance of Chaplain Craig, that I have an unhealthy need for attention. This unhealthy belief led me to hurt people, and I was about to get put back in front of people. As I was internalizing this, it allowed me to begin my process of taking inventory of not only my feelings, but also of my motives and agenda.

At this point in my journey, I knew my goal was to create opportunities to connect families and give men a chance to share hope and love with their loved ones, and I especially wanted to focus on situations that would showcase Jesus. I also put an emphasis on promoting love and togetherness with a goal of changing the prison atmosphere and culture at SQSP and in DOC. Even though I knew my goals and had my agenda clearly identified, I still had little experience in giving God glory while speaking and being in front of men rather than putting myself on the pedestal. I am grateful, happy, and overjoyed by the program's impact on the men, their families, and the staff for the time I got to be involved. There were on average more than 140 men who faithfully showed up each Saturday afternoon, choosing to sing, worship, and hear about God rather than go to the yard, the library, or any of the other things people do while in prison. Along with that, dozens of volunteers came in weekly to share their life and remind all of us that we are loved and not forgotten.

God doesn't waste a thing.

# 16

As I reflect on all my years in prison, I am fond of the time I had setting up and tearing down for GBB, and I am very grateful to have been a part of something so special. See, in prison, alone time is very rare to come by, and this was another blessing that appeared when we began this program. Mark, Kyle, and I would show up every Saturday to set up the service during the 11:00 a.m. count and lockdown time. We would have the service, then we would stay through the 4:00 p.m. lockdown time as well. It was these two hours every week when the three of us could get away, if needed, for quiet time and prayer or just have a peaceful moment where we could shut off the worries and loudness of the facility. These hours also became a great time to learn as Mark and Kyle had been walking with the Lord much longer than I had. I would sit with them and ask questions, debate with them, and ultimately absorb as much as I could about Jesus, the Bible, or even just how to survive in prison following Christ. Mark was now going on his twenty-seventh consecutive year in DOC, and Kyle was on his thirteenth. These days were precious and yet another example of God continually showing up in small and big moments. He will not let a count time go by without putting a blessing on it.

God doesn't waste a thing.

# 17

It was during this time when Chaplain Craig began a training program for men from the streets who had a calling and a passion to come into the Department of Corrections to become a chaplain. This mentorship Craig was about to pilot had me excited because if he was vouching for and training this person, then I just knew he was going to be great and loving. I had no idea, however, how life-changing the relationships that grew from this program would be on me, in prison and once released. Craig introduced me to the first apprentice in California prison history, Jameson, and I tell you what, he had a true passion and heart for men in prison. Jameson was faithful, he was steadfast, and he based his decisions on what was said in the Bible and if it aligned with the Word of the Lord, and ultimately, that is what led his life. This was inspiring to me. I was able to see someone younger than me, completely bought in for Jesus, trusting in the Holy Spirit for guidance. I reflect often on my time with Jameson. I see it as God showing me, no matter the differences in how people were raised, the similarities far outweigh them when you have Jesus in common. Jameson grew up in a conservative anabaptist community when he then made the difficult decision to go against his family's and the community's traditional beliefs. Jameson, instead, chose to run to the Cross and focus more on his relationship with Christ while following the calling he had to prison ministry.

This always gave me confidence. As is often in prison, there is a "popular" and "status quo" way of doing your time, and it rarely aligned with the Word of God. The idea of separating yourself from your family and community, knowing it could have a significant impact on all relationships yet still choosing to chase after Jesus, reinforced to me I could let the Holy Spirit be my guide, whether the prison population agreed with me or chose to look down on me. I knew I could always get honesty, consistency, and an answer rooted in biblical truth when I sat down to chat with Jameson. I could also get a tough game of chess while hearing of a few fishing stories from this brother of mine.

God doesn't waste a thing.

# 18

With the success Jameson had as the program's first apprentice, it opened the door for another man of God to train under Craig. Let me tell you how great our God is: When He sees an opportunity to bless His kids, He sure exceeds all our wildest expectations as He prepared for me to have a new lifelong brother and best friend walk into the chapel.

It's Christmastime 2015, and I have now been working in the chapel for about six months, and I am in a very confused headspace. I was struggling with my identity and with anger toward what I did and how my life had turned out. I would spend much of my day helping others in the chapel feel valued and loved while going back to my cell at night and feeling worthless and lonely. I could help people throughout the day work through their fears while sitting in Craig's office in tears. I could not come to grips on what I needed to do to be set spiritually free myself. I know this sounds like two totally different sets of thoughts and feelings, and it was. I was all over the board, spiritually seeking healing but not yet willing to let go of what had me so mad. I was like a dog with a bone, only the bone was my fear and my overall struggle with identity and forgiveness. Most of all I felt alone, and I missed my first real friend, my brother Lee. Before I move on from here to how God worked it out, I need to say Lee was, and is, a great brother and an even more phenomenal father to his two sons. Any anger I carried toward Lee during my seven years was because I was judging him off my unrealistic expectations and how often I felt he should visit. I was neglecting to take ownership of the truth that my choice not only sent me to prison, but it also ripped away from Lee his little brother, his friend, the uncle to his boys, and his sense of family unity, all in one fail swoop. Not to mention the burden of looking out for our parents was now solely placed on his shoulders while I was gone.

Back to Christmastime—I am sitting in the chapel eagerly waiting for Craig to come in with the new apprentice candidate. Mark and I were going over Joseph and his relationship with his brothers. This is one of my favorite stories in the Bible as he was constantly covered in God's love, and over time God used the tragedy in Joseph's situation to further His kingdom's mission. Mark is chatting away, and I look through the window to see Craig walking into the chapel, followed by an athletic-looking man with a smile on his face from ear to ear. This man carried himself with a confidence not common inside of a prison, especially for someone who is coming into SQSP for the first time. I later learned and can attribute the confidence not to who he is and how he feels but rather the confidence he has in his Lord and Savior Jesus.

Craig walked in and introduced Mark and me to Trent. And I can say, with no reservations, from the first handshake, I knew I just met someone real special. I am shaking hands with someone God wanted in my life, someone who would not just be a friend, but also a best friend and brother for the rest of my life. Trent did not replace my brother; I am not saying that in any way. But God did graft the two of us together in a way that still to this day leaves me speechless. Where I saw a loss of a brother's presence, God saw it as an opportunity to bless me with another.

God doesn't waste a thing.

CHAPTER

# 19

It is important to note here there were many men I came in contact within DOC who had a positive impact on my life. But a short list of them had a true, life-altering one. Chaplain Craig, of course, is up there, just below my father as the most inspirational and influential man in my life. Paul, from Mule Creek, will always be special as he showed what integrity and character looks like, in person and in business. Trent Seton also makes that list as he showed me what it's like to be all in for Jesus, not to mention he had balance in the other areas of his life, with a passion for family, friends, sports, and even *The Dan Patrick Show*. He and I connected on all the above from day one and are still as close as brothers to this day. We enjoy God, golf, good laughs, family, and of course, *The Dan Patrick Show*. One of the perks of working in the chapel was this access and the time that was made available to sit and learn from Craig, Jameson, and Trent.

A bonus to the ministry that supports all three of these chaplains, which is New Hope Ministry (NHM), is that they love to come into prisons and play sports against the men who are incarcerated. I like to joke, on most days, Craig and his buddies like to come into prison to tell us that we are loved and that God has not forgotten about us. But on the days when he would bring a team in for either volleyball, basketball, or softball, they would come in and dominate us and encourage us through the tough love of Jesus. It needs to be highlighted Craig would bring in his son, Andrew, to play us in all these sports, and often it would end with a prisoner not being able to get out of the way of a volleyball spiked into his chest, knocking the wind out of him. These teams were good, and they had no problem in outplaying us most days, all while showing great sportsmanship and building relationships that build character and love throughout the facilities. I can remember vividly the first time I played softball against Trent at San Quentin. I witnessed him diving for a ball in the outfield then getting up and throwing a runner out at third. His defensive skills were astonishing, but it was the way he hit a softball that left the men inside speechless. He hit one so far that it not only went out of the field, but it also ended up hitting one of the cell houses outside of the rec yard. The next day, after this softball beating, I found Craig and asked him if he looks for apprentices who can hit a softball a mile or ones who love Jesus. His reply was "They can both exist together." You know what? He was right.

The more time I spent with Trent, the more I knew I had much to learn from him. It is often said, if you want to know what your future will look like, look at your friends. Reflecting on that comment and truth, I knew my future would be better with Trent in it. He lives by biblical truths and has a great way of accepting compliments as he receives them with gratitude then acknowledges it is all God, giving Him the glory. Trent has a saying I have since adopted as has several of my friends inside DOC, and it is "If it looks like Jesus …," implying if it's an action, an attitude, or an approach to treating others, do your best to look like Jesus in that moment. Jesus is the gold standard, a standard we can never achieve. But a close miss to treating others like Jesus is a blessed encounter still. "IILLJ" is a great set of letters to focus on in your daily walk.

God doesn't waste a thing.

# 20

I have heard it stated before, there is not a book large enough to encompass all the miracles Jesus did while walking on this earth. This book is much the same; there is not enough pages to explain all the ways I witnessed God do a miracle through my time at SQSP and beyond, some of them personally in my life and situation and others I was blessed to be a part of and witness with my own two eyes. I remember, when I was three years old, running down the hallway at my Grandma Belt's house, going to see Grandpa. When I got to his office, there were what looked like hundreds of pages of paper thrown all over the floor, containing what were his best efforts to write his name correctly. Out of the corner of his eye, he spotted me, turned, and yelled, "Who are you?"

I ran away crying. That was my first encounter with Alzheimer's disease and the effects of dementia. It was horrifying, and sad, and I knew I didn't want to be around it or feel it. Fast forward thirty-four years, I am sitting in the chapel with Mark talking, when Craig walks in and said he got it approved to have a special Friday worship service, when the Muslims were in the chapel for their service. Craig and Mark had discussed this idea, and it had been approved. Their idea was we would go down to the dementia pod and sing to the men with this disease who were incarcerated.

As uncomfortable as I knew this would make me, I trusted the hearts of Craig and Mark, and so I tagged along to the dementia pod to sing worship with them.

We would go down there every Friday; Craig, Mark, Trent, Jameson, and myself carrying a couple of guitars and an amplifier, ready to sing and praise Jesus. It was a lot of fun, and sometimes others would join in as well. The nurses of the pod would participate, which added a different dynamic to their relationship with the men they were helping. We got reports that the attitudes in the pod began to change as well as the climate they were living in. So we kept going. Every Friday we would pray with them when we got there, sing for them, and pray for them when we left, and repeat. Pray, sing, pray. Pray, sing, pray. What I started out not wanting to do turned into one of my most cherished times and favorite things to do, but that's not the cool part.

One man who had lived in that pod for years, Mr. Grey, had not spoken for over three years. He didn't respond to questions. He wouldn't tell you his name. He never uttered a comment or even a grunt. Nothing. It was sad. All he did was sit in his wheelchair, rub his head, and pat his stomach. Prior to this lifestyle, Mr. Grey was one of the best legal minds the Department of Corrections had ever seen, and now he couldn't even tell you what his name was. I would go up to him every Friday and ask him how he was doing and if he was ready to worship Jesus. Each time he would sit quietly without any reaction whatsoever. The nurses who worked there told me numerous times he didn't understand what I was saying and that I was wasting my time speaking to him. As my mom and all my friends will tell you, I don't need a response for me to talk to someone; I will talk to a wall. But I got what she was saying, and I guess I just liked the idea of letting him know I was there for him. It must have been four to five months of all of us going there every Friday to sing, when one afternoon Craig, Trent, Mark, Jameson, and myself began to sing "Amazing Grace," as we often did. Only this time we witnessed a miracle. During the chorus, we had an extra voice join in! With tears running down his cheeks, Mr. Grey was singing. He was singing every word. He didn't miss one. It was amazing. I looked at the others to see if they were witnessing this, and they were. I could barely sing as I was crying at the beautiful sight of what the Holy Spirit was doing in this moment. Tears were falling from everyone there because this miracle did not just bless Mr. Grey, but it also blessed us all. Dementia may have taken this man's body, but his soul belonged to God. From that encounter, one of the nurses gave her life to the Lord. Praise God. God won't let an opportunity go by to bring His children home. If He needed to use a man who hadn't spoken in over a thousand days to open the eyes of that one nurse, well, consider it quiet time well spent.

God doesn't waste a thing.

# 21

Around the prison, I was doing my best to see God in everyday encounters because I realized the same God who empowers the mute to sing is the same God who calls us to treat our neighbor with love. My focus became those around me as I became more committed to the ME 3 lifestyle. I was going to become intentional about being present for those individuals directly in front of me. This helped me align my heart with that of a servant and being available for those in my circle of influence. It was around this time Grandma Belt was deteriorating rapidly health-wise as the end of her life was coming near. This reality upset me as I was about to lose one of my favorite people in this world, who also happened to be my greatest supporter and prayer warrior.

Grandma had gotten to the point she was no longer aware of who the people around her were and had little knowledge of her whereabouts. It was common for her to look directly at my mother, her daughter, and ask her who she was and what she was doing near her. In the middle of July, I was able to get a call from my pops while I was working in the chapel with Craig, who had arranged for this phone call. Everyone thought this would be the last time I would get to speak to Grandma and get closure. I was sitting in Craig's office with him, talking to my dad on speaker phone, when I heard my dad tell me, "Son, she is having a real bad day," and he reminded me she hasn't really spoken in the last week other than to ask what we are doing in her room.

He then told me I should just focus on telling her I love her, keep it brief, and not expect too much. Grandma gets on the phone, and I say, "Hi, Grandma, it's me, Lukey," and she comes to life.

She begins asking me questions about prison and working in the chapel. She asks how I am feeling and if I am still studying the book of John, which was always her favorite book. She then told me how proud of me she is and she loves me. It was incredible. It was the best gift I could have ever asked for as I got to tell Grandma I loved her and missed her. After I told her goodbye, my dad got back on the phone, and he was speechless. It was the first time she had spoken like that in months. It was a gift from God, and I am so thankful for that talk as she passed away a few days later, on July 20, 2016. God invented reconciliation and family, and He wasn't going to miss a chance to bring Grandma and me together one last time. A prison wall wasn't going to get in the way of that.

God doesn't waste a thing.

CHAPTER

# 22

There was a seminar Chaplain Craig put on every year at SQSP with volunteers Larry and his wife Jan, who are two of the most earnest and faithful prayer warriors I have ever met. These two are small in stature and tenderhearted, yet they go deep into the pain and fear that binds men up in spiritual warfare. This program was called Bondage to Freedom and was designed to create a safe place for men to break free from what is holding them back from living in the victory of our Lord Jesus Christ. The seminar had several breakout sessions, where the men participating were invited to dig deep, be vulnerable, and take the wound that hurt the most, the one we try the hardest to keep secret from others, even ourselves, and renounce its power. This was done by laying it down at the foot of the Cross, giving it to Jesus, all while being supported and prayed over by the others in the seminar. I watched men, hardened men, gang members, share their shame, in conjunction with them dropping to their knees, crying out to the Lord for healing. These men had tears falling from their eyes, tears of joy, tears of release, tears that only come from a breakthrough.

For three straight years, I helped set this up yet never entered the battle for myself. I was there supporting and praying with my buddies as they entered war and came out victorious, and I would choose to return to my seat of safety, back by Trent, and not allow myself to be vulnerable. Craig would come sit by me and walk with me, telling me, "It's OK," while encouraging me it's time to fight my fear, share my truth, and take back my freedom.

Each time his kindness was met with me saying, "Nope, I can't do that."

The last two times people found out about my past and my truth, I came face-to-face with knives while getting my life threatened. Craig never pushed or was rude, neither was Jameson, Trent, nor Mark. I remember Craig sharing with me two things that day: one was I was loved and not alone, and the other was the power was in the secret. Sadly, I admit all three seminars came and went, and I never did feel total freedom at San Quentin.

SQSP is considered a medical facility, and just as we would go down to the dementia pod to sing to those men, we would also go up to the hospice unit and sing to those who were sick and injured. I was not thrilled about going into hospice. It made me uncomfortable, and I didn't do well with sickness and death. Knowing this, the chaplains would let me know this isn't about me, and God was not as concerned about my comfort as He was with me going to bless others who are in a worse situation than I was. Thankfully, my stubbornness didn't win out, and the encouragement of the chaplains took me out of my comfort zone, where I could be present to witness a mighty miracle. One day, while Mark and I were working in the chapel, Craig got a call from one of the nurses, asking for him to come up to the hospice unit as quickly as possible. When we got up there, we were led to the room of Mr. Baker, who was a very angry God-hating man. Mr. Baker had been in hospice for over a year because of the number of surgeries he had put himself through. You see, he would eat all sorts of things, from TV remote controls to razors, batteries, and even the metal from the fire sprinklers in the ceiling. He did this to force DOC to do surgery and spend money on keeping him alive. When Craig entered the room, he began asking Mr. Baker if there was anything he could do for him. Mark and I peeked into the room, while Craig was being told, in quite colorful language, God is not real, and we saw this man had a hole in his stomach that could not heal from all the surgeries. This hole must have been two to three inches in diameter. I remember it was large enough to set a soda can inside of it.

These few facts set the stage for what will forever be one of the most life-changing moments I have ever heard and seen. While Craig was in the room with Mr. Baker, recognizing his life was coming to an end, he asked him if he would like to hear about Jesus and form a relationship with the one true God. This question was met with a blank stare and a not-so-subtle "No!" To which Craig asked if it would be all right if he prays for him. Mr. Baker fired back, "If it makes you feel better, holy man, go ahead."

So Craig raised his hand and began to pray over him. Craig was asking for the Lord to reveal himself clearly to this man and to let him know he is loved. I am listening to this prayer from the hallway, when I hear Craig pray to the Lord to heal this man and restore the hole in his stomach back to perfection. As we were getting ready to walk back to the chapel, I whisper to Mark, somewhat sarcastically, "Did Craig just pray for a three-inch hole to be healed and restored? That's ridiculous!"

No more than two days later, Craig gets another call from the nurse, saying he needs to come back up to Mr. Baker's room. I am totally thinking he must have passed away, and Craig needs to go do the legal work necessary for a death notification. When we get up there, we enter the room of a completely different, transformed Mr. Baker. He is smiling, full of joy, his eyes are lit, and he is shouting to Craig, "Jesus is real!"

He lifts his shirt to show Craig the hole in his stomach has been healed. It's covered with skin—real skin. The same hole no doctor could heal, no number of staples or stitches could connect—skin. It's important to stress this was all the work of the God, the Mighty Healer and Great Physician, not any special combination of words Craig said in his prayer. Later that day, Craig led him in a prayer, and he gave his life to the Lord. Amen.

God can do whatever He wants, whenever He wants, and He will use anybody necessary to accomplish His goal of reuniting men and women back to Himself. From Mr. Baker's miracle came more fruit than just himself giving his life to the Lord. There were a couple of inmates who worked up in the hospice unit, who did not believe in the Lord, but just witnessed this man being healed, and they didn't know what to do with that fact. No medicine was changed, no secret surgery took place, even the doctors didn't know how to explain this event. The only thing it could have been was God, and that doesn't sit well with unbelievers. A couple of those inmates wrestled with this new experience and wound up sitting in Craig's office, with the Cross on the floor, and tears soaking the carpet as they also gave their lives to Lord. God's not going to let a sprinkler-eating, battery-digesting man go unused in His plan of making heaven more crowded.

God doesn't waste a thing.

# 23

This, however, was not the end of Mr. Baker's story. He was much like Saul in the Bible, had a drastic change of heart moment and was not going to keep it to himself. He told everyone within shouting distance about God and what He can, has, and will do. Through this zeal for sharing the Lord, he ruffled some feathers within the unit as he would not sugarcoat his new relationship with Jesus. He ended up being sent to another facility because one of the nurses retaliated against him when he told her that she wouldn't be so mean if she found Jesus, which is funny but true. However, that was just too much truth for her. Often, for nonbelievers, the truth can hurt and tends to lead to a sense of being uncomfortable.

About a year later, Mr. Baker became deathly ill and was returned to SQSP as he needed constant hospice care as his health deteriorated. Craig had the opportunity to go and sit with him a few hours every so often, and he was just as on fire for the Lord as when he left. The next thing God had planned for Mr. Baker wasn't uniquely put in place for himself. He had already witnessed his own "hole-healing" miracle; his next journey was for those around him. If there is a soul to save and a heart to restore, God will not pass up a moment to do so. And He did this exact thing through Mr.

Baker going into a coma. One of the nurses had to be present with him the entire time he was in his coma, per DOC policy, as there needs to be a witness to when the exact time of death was. While he was in his coma, this one nurse would sing songs of praise in the room and pray for God's peace and will to be done in his situation.

While he was going in and out of consciousness, he spoke, and what he said moved the nurse to call for Craig immediately. Craig got up there, and she told him what she heard him say, and they agreed, if he woke up again, they would share with him what he uttered, which is exactly what happened. Once awake and cognizant of what was going on, Craig asked him if he remembered speaking to the nurse, and he said, "No, what did I say?"

Craig and the nurse moved closer to him and told him that he said, "It's so beautiful, it's so peaceful, why did I have to come back?"

Mr. Baker had no recollection of those comments but looked at Craig and asked him, "Why did I have to come back?"

Craig did not know how to respond; he didn't know why this happened. However, the nurse chimed in and said, "You came back for me. I needed to hear that because I was feeling empty, and what you experienced and said filled my tank and restored my soul."

Mr. Baker died shortly after that conversation. He returned home peacefully.

God doesn't waste a thing, not even a comment made during a coma.

# 24

There were several constants during my chaplain clerk years, but none more consistent and persistent than my buddy Mark. We would sit in the office every day for hours on end, joking, laughing, studying, reading, sometimes arguing, but always ending the day coming together praying. So it didn't come as a surprise to me that my heart ached when Mark began to show signs of sickness as his body continued to give in brought about by all the years of wear and tear from living the way he did in prison. Mark knew this was coming. He was the first to admit there were consequences to living a hard life for nearly forty years. Toward the end of a rough day, when I was in my feelings and having myself a pity party, Mark asked if I would sit down so we could talk. The next conversation was one of the most influential talks I have had in my life.

Mark asked me a simple question that led to a very complex discussion, which ended in a life-changing answer. Mark asked, "Luke, who is Jesus to you?"

I looked at him and said, "Jesus is my Savior." I said it with such confidence as if I had just aced a test because up to that point, I believed that was who Jesus was to me.

For the next hour, Mark and I spoke, and many of the details I will choose to keep private as they are special to me, but Mark led me in a heartfelt discussion about Jesus being more than that and that life will look different, I will act different, I will pray different, and I will want different, when I choose to accept Jesus as my personal Lord. It was this day that I made my Lordship decision and moved my life toward a daily walk to live according to God's will, not my will. It is said, when we accept Jesus as our Savior, that moment impacts one, but proclaiming Jesus as our Lord, that impacts everyone around us. Mark lovingly explained the difference between the two and shared the moment he heard from God on a personal prayer about his brother, which led to his Lordship proclamation. This chat left an everlasting mark on me and pretty much everywhere I stepped foot after that, not just spiritually, but also physically as I would write the letters NMW everywhere I went, on anything I could, to remind myself it is "Not My Will" I seek, but the Lord's. Not My Will became the inspiration of my very own ministry once I was released from prison, and I owe much of it to Mark for the knowledge and inspiration to seek the will of the Lord daily.

A couple of weeks after that talk, Mark was severely showing signs of adult jaundice as his skin and the whites in his eyes were turning yellow. He was carrying lots of extra weight in his stomach from the bloating, and he now walked with a limp from the swelling in his legs and ankles. All this was out of the ordinary as Mark was always in shape, and the only color on his skin was the color of the many tattoos. He continued to lead worship, guitar resting on his stomach, as a slight grimace crept up on his face. He wouldn't tell anyone of his pain, but behind closed doors, he cried. He grieved as he knew what was coming. He was not scared about dying. He was sad about leaving the people he cared about and loved. He always told me he thought of me as a little brother and that he loved me, and I could feel he meant it. Mark was devastated he was eventually going to have to tell Chaplain Craig goodbye. See, the thing was Craig was Mark's favorite person in the world; even though Mark was older, he revered Craig and admired how he carried himself. Mark told me in private many times Craig was one of maybe three people who always believed in him and loved him.

One night, while Mark was sleeping, no more than forty feet away from me in Cell House 7, a vein in Mark's throat ruptured, and he bled all over the cell floor. His roommate got an officer, and they got him into an ambulance from the prison and to a hospital as quickly as possible. We later learned this is called esophageal varices. Mark got to the emergency room, and he was coming in and out of consciousness for a while until the doctor's decided to put him into a medically induced coma. Obviously, I was not allowed to go to the hospital to see him for security reasons. However, Chaplain Craig got notified of Mark's situation and headed to the hospital. When he got there, he saw the doctors and nurses tending to him, and Mark had been placed inside of a hyperbaric chamber to better his chances of healing. Craig then headed off to a waiting room, where he sat down and prayed to God for healing and to bring Mark back. Craig shared, while he was praying, he heard from God say, "Mark is not going to die, but I am going to work on his heart while he is out."

A few days later, Mark awoke from his coma and was stable from the surgeries and could come back to SQSP. The first visitor to see Mark was Craig. As he entered the room, Mark had a large smile on his face, which itself is a blessing, considering the pain and trauma he was going through. When Mark saw Craig, he told him, "I have got something I need to tell you!"

Craig jumped in and said, "I already know, God told me in prayer that you weren't going to die but that he was going to work on your heart."

Mark, amazed at this revelation, said, "That is correct, he did work on my heart, but there is more."

Mark was now back in Cell House 7, where he and I lived, and he was moving slowly from the surgeries. Craig informed him that morning he was not allowed to come to work in the chapel and he was to stay in his room and get better. This resting time off was supported by the administration, and as far as prison terms go, this was considered a direct order for Mark to take it easy. Craig also made me aware of this order, that Mark was not allowed to come work, but I knew Mark. Mark was a man who would follow rules, especially ones coming from Craig, but not ones that kept him from sharing Jesus and a miracle.

As expected, that evening, when Craig had left for the day and I had the Bible study all set up for the evening, I looked out the window and saw Mark slowly making his way down the twenty stairs from Cell House 7 to the chapel. When he got into the office, I gave him a big hug and told him I knew Craig told him he was not allowed in the chapel to work, to which he replied, "I am not working, you are. I am just going to sit here and talk to you."

Mark shut the door so we would not be interrupted by the study going on in the chapel, and he told me God sent him back because he had a message for me. I was speechless. Two or three years ago, I would have thought this was nonsense, but having seen and lived through so many miracles up to this point, I knew I was about to hear something I needed to comprehend. Mark told me that while he was in his coma, he met his angel, and he said, "Luke, angels are huge, and they fill up an entire corner of the room."

Mark followed that up with this next statement: "Luke, I met your angel too, and he is ginormous. He told me to tell you that he is always with you, and he is always ready. All you need to do is call on him. He's waiting, he just needs you to invite him into your situations."

To tell you I was weeping would be an understatement. I was so overcome with emotions and joy that I couldn't even form a sentence. Mark grabbed my hands and told me he knew I would be fine, but there were going to be times ahead when I was going to need to call on my angel and trust in God. I will never forget that night and those words, and I am grateful Mark chose to come down that evening to share that with me as I wasn't even around SQSP for another week.

God doesn't waste a thing.

# 25

I t's now the first week of February 2017, and I am sleeping comfortably, well, as much as possible on the top bunk of a metal slab, with a seventy-year-old snoring underneath me. It's at this time when I'm awoken by five loud kicks on my door and two officers screaming, "Chance, get up!"

I jump down, open the door, and am told I need to pack my stuff up, that I am moving facilities in fifty minutes. With panic in my eyes, I begin to argue with them. I tell them they must have the wrong person. I work in the chapel, and I don't want to leave. They let me rant for a while then repeated once again, "Chance, you are leaving this facility, and now you only have forty minutes, so you better begin to pack your property."

I am crying as I am trying to pack up my property while reality sets in that I am not going to see my friends again. I can't say bye to Mark, Craig, Trent, Jameson, Kyle, Davis, Stan, and the list goes on and on. Then it hits me—I am about to go somewhere again, where I know nobody, and the possibility of being killed is creeping back into my mind. I still hadn't realized or taken the time to piece together that I went through this same process when I asked to go to protective custody but instead got sent here, a place where I am now acting the same way, not wanting to leave, not recognizing the blessing it turned out to be. I am sad, mad, scared, rushed, and now it is time to go.

As I push my bag down to the property room, I am totally convinced this is wrong; it's a mistake, and I can't go. I was good thinking I would stay here at San Quentin for fifteen more years, until 2032. I'm comfortable, I'm safe, and I'm witnessing God do miracle after miracle. I am talking to friends who are seeing angels that have messages for me, hearing from chaplains who get direct words from God in prayer. I have seen a man sing after not saying a word in over three years and seeing bodies heal no medical professional can explain. I don't want to miss out on any of these things. I don't want to leave where God is at. Here I am, once again, arguing with God I know what is best, not mature enough to stop, breathe, and pray in moments of crisis.

I'm now down at the property building, with five other guys who are leaving today, and I am bringing up any excuse to having to step inside the building to get my property accounted for. I am dropping socks and shirts out of my bag on purpose to slow the process down in hopes Craig will be on time this morning. I see Craig walk through the door, and I whistle up to him to get his attention, and he looks down and sees me. He shouts and asks if I need a "ride" back up to the chapel, not realizing yet I am being shipped out of the facility. I get Craig down to where I'm at. The tears that had stopped have now begun again as I am now hearing myself say goodbye and that I'm leaving while also begging him to stop this. I plead to him, "Go find someone, Craig, make this stop!"

At this time, I am no longer able to ignore what's happening, and I'm pulled inside the property building, and the door shuts as it's now my time to get packed out. I begin the process of logging all my socks, boxer briefs, TV, razors, etc. This is always one of the humbling parts of living in prison, when your entire pile of property fits into a trash bag and a two-foot-by-three-foot storage box. I bag it, sign it, and push it to the transportation area.

Next thing that happens is I am put into a prison-orange jumpsuit inmates get put into when they are being transported. I am being handcuffed, shackled, black-boxed, and chained up for the bus ride, when I see Craig walk in. Now black-boxed, for your reference, is when they overlap your hands, palm to palm, and handcuff them through a box so you cannot move your wrists at all, other than to touch your own wrists. Honestly, it is probably a good thing they were immovable at this point because of the next thing that happens. When I see Craig, I notice he is not smiling. As a matter of fact, it is the most upset I have seen him. He said the word he uses when he's super angry. He said, "Luke, this has me grouchy! I can't do anything. Nobody I spoke with even knew this was happening."

This was odd as the lieutenant, the captain, the major, or the warden were not aware of this move as normally one, if not all, would have known and told Craig. He told me this was bigger than all of them and that it must be God, which brings on a conversation I will never forget.

I now realized nobody could help me. Nobody was getting me off this bus; I am leaving. Craig told me, "Luke, it's going to be fine, it's time for you to go there and grow and help others."

I followed that up with "Nope, it's not going to work out, I'm safe here!" And now I am crying again, which, to be honest and clear, is not a good look in prison, especially when boarding a bus to go to a whole new yard. Nothing says "easy target" like a crying, whimpering new guy stepping off the bus.

Craig put his hand on my shoulder, looked me right in the eyes, and asked, "Luke, do you trust God?"

I begrudgingly said, "Yeah," and he asked then, "Does God make mistakes?"

Here, I replied very sarcastically, "Not yet, but look at your watch because He is about to."

Craig followed that up with the thing I didn't want to hear. He said, "Luke, all things work together for good—"

I cut him off, "Don't tell me that now, Craig."

Honestly, if I wasn't handcuffed, I would have tried to hit him because that is not the verse you want to hear when you are about to go through a rough time or you just received bad news. Romans 8:28 is one of those verses that does not always feel good. Craig smiled and said, "Feelings don't change the truth. We may not like the way this feels, but it doesn't make God and His promise to us less true." He then prayed for me. I am now being escorted to the bus.

When I look back, Craig told me he will come see me in a few months and to trust God. And like that, I am gone. My San Quentin time is over. Off to Folsom, where I hope I don't die and don't know if God will show up for me there. My time at WSP was not wasted as it got me to SQSP, and He didn't waste my three years while at SQSP, so once again, let's see what His plan is going to be for me at my next stop.

God doesn't waste a thing.

# 26

Walking into Folsom State Prison, February 2017, I realized one thing right away—it was huge. If there were approximately eight hundred to nine hundred people at SQSP, there were now an additional seven hundred to eight hundred men here with me at FSP. I remember thinking to myself, *Am I going to be scared, and is this going to be miserable with all these people, or am I going to mature, lean into God, and grow my faith while making this the best place while I am here?*

I tried to find the positive and told myself there were so many people to share God with and help promote love and change and let time tell the story.

After a few days of getting moved through the intake unit, I get called in and told I am moving to Cell House 8 on the east side of the complex. Cell Houses 7 and 8 are often referred to as the "Thunderdome" units because of its size, its layout, and certainly, its volume. I was told this was the best option available as the east side was where the incentive pods were. It's where more men were trying to stay out of trouble and less youngsters getting in the mix. Cell House 8 was huge; it had three hundred people living in a hundred a fifty rooms. The unit consisted of three floors, with twenty-five rooms on each side of each floor, and it was loud. At first glance, it looked scary and intimidating but was not a bad spot after I got into a groove, met a couple of people, and began to figure out my routine. It was within my first two weeks there that I was able to step right into God's first miracle there.

Without sounding entitled and spoiled, I really wasn't looking forward to having to go work in the kitchen, which is the standard job placement at any prison when you arrive. I was blessed and didn't have to work in the kitchen at SQSP as I was brought there to teach GED, but I wasn't thinking about that. I was fearful it would be like it was at Mule Creek, with threats and a job counting out dinner rolls. Not that this is as large as some of the miracles and blessings I have already experienced and will experience in the future, but this was a huge relief and great start or, rather, continuation of the work God was doing in my life. Not that I am comparing myself to Joseph, that is for others to compare, but there sure are similarities where God's favor was "with me" wherever I went. Saying all that, it's clear to see I did not get hired in the kitchen. Instead, I got hired in the library, where the librarian recognized me from teaching GED at SQSP, where he was working as the part-time librarian for a brief period. Thank God he did not waste a chance encounter three years ago. The benefits of this job in the library, over the time in the kitchen, is more than just avoiding cutting onions and counting rolls; it also was the setup to my success over the remainder of my time at Folsom.

One day, as I was working in the library, I got called back to the librarian's office, where, inside, I met Captain P, who oversaw all programs in the facility as well as the library. Also sitting in the office was Sergeant Stenson, who happened to be over all the volunteers in the recreation department and bringing in teams from the community to play the prison teams. When I step inside the office, Captain P asked if I was the Chance who came over from San Quentin. I told her yes, and she followed it up by asking if I knew anything about the San Quentin newsletter they were putting together there at SQSP. Again, I told her yes and that, in fact, I was the main editor and did all the proofreading for the newsletter, along with doing my main role at SQSP, which was working in the chapel for Craig. Sergeant Stenson looks up and confirms I know Craig, and he then tells me he knows Craig well. Turns out, he played softball against him in the Canon City leagues and works with him to bring in the New Hope team to play us in the different sports. From this quick chat, God had managed to connect me with two of the most impactful people at FSP in terms of things I am interested in. Captain P informed me she and FSP were looking to create their own newsletter and asked if I would not only be willing to help, but also invited me to join this team of guys who have been at FSP for years. Many of these men are still great friends of mine, and the way God put us together shortened the process for how people become friends in prison by many months. I said yes to her offer. God's timing is never late and never early; it is always perfect. As far as Sergeant Stenson and how my life changed in rec, well, there is plenty more to that story later.

God doesn't waste a thing.

# 27

A couple of months into my time at Folsom, I get told Chaplain Craig and his guys were going to be coming in to play volleyball against the offenders. I was excited to see him and some familiar faces. I just knew he would bring Trent and his son, Andrew, who never missed a chance to come play us and destroy us in all sports. The facility called movement to the gym, and I remember thinking how happy I was to get to go see Craig again. As I was running into the gym from the yard, Craig was standing, waiting in the doorway for me to come in. As soon as I did, he saw I was smiling, which led him to smile, shake my hand, as we were not allowed to hug, and he asked me one question: "Is Romans 8:28 true?"

I took a second and said, "Yes, of course!"

We go sit down to chat and catch up as he can clearly see all things have begun to work together for good, and joining us in this chat is Trent. Life was great in this moment.

The three of us were sitting there chatting while some of the others from NHM were playing. Craig informed me he had figured out what had happened at SQSP and why I got moved without anybody knowing. It turned out it was the decision of one lady, who happened to be my case manager, and that she was uncomfortable with the amount of Christian support and love I was receiving throughout the facility and from the volunteers who came in for Bible studies and services. Craig told me he could move me back if I wanted to, but it would take about six months for that to happen. I told him not to worry about it, and Craig agreed. Neither of us knew yet what God had planned for me at Folsom, but we knew I was supposed to be at FSP for this season. God had shown himself to be faithful and wise in all circumstances, and He was not going to waste a jealous case manager in furthering His plan in my life and the lives of those around me.

God doesn't waste a thing.

# 28

Another couple of months had passed, and during this time, I get the sad news that Mark Foster had passed away. This was terrible news for me. But it was also some news I could rejoice in as I knew Mark no longer felt pain and was now serving a much different and joyful life sentence. I could smile knowing he got to kill his DOC number California used for twenty-eight years to identify him by as he was reborn into God's house. He was no longer identified by a number but a resident of heaven living in the presence of the Lord.

Timing could not have been better as a few weeks later, Chaplain Craig brought his team back to FSP, only this time to play basketball. As I was sitting on Craig's bench, talking to him and a few of the guys he brought in, Sergeant Stenson came by and told Craig he was a couple of referees short, so Craig volunteered me to ref for a bit. It was that moment where Craig told Sergeant Stenson I would be a great help for him anywhere needed in the rec department. The following week, Sergeant Stenson called me into his office in the gym and gave me a rec "volunteer pass," which allowed me to go to any yard or gym at any time. This pass was very rare. There were maybe only twenty men in the whole facility who had one. The norm was you had to have helped with three seasons of sports over a three-year span to be eligible to get one. I got one after five months of being at the facility.

Living in Cell House 8 was loud, it was dirty, and many of the guys there were disrespectful, which is common for any cell house. I was beginning to make friends, and all things considered, I was doing well; however, I wanted to get moved to unit 6-Upper, which was an incentive unit with less people, bigger rooms, and no toilets in the individual rooms. It was like the rooms I was living in at SQSP, which is best described as a terrible college dorm, and that is what I wanted. The rule at Folsom was someone needed to be write-up free for one year at that facility before being eligible to live in 6-Upper. However, God had a different criterion for me, and I was moved up there after only six months. This move began some great times with some unbelievably awesome lifelong friends.

I remember walking around the four different pods in 6-Upper (pods A, B, C, and D) and feeling there was a guy God was telling me to go talk to, so I bought two Diet Cokes and walked up to him and asked him if he wanted one. He told me, "Even though Dr. Pepper is my favorite, I will gladly take it."

That Diet Coke began a friendship with Sammy that is still amazing to this day. Through Sammy, I met so many other friends. I joined a softball team called the Fowl Balls, which was comprised of guys trying to make their lives and DOC better by doing the right things. Sammy also helped me land a job essential to me leaving a legacy in DOC. That Diet Coke was not wasted on Sammy.

God doesn't waste a thing.

# 29

As I had mentioned earlier, getting moved to 6-Upper was one of the most pivotal events that affected my living situation as well as my social situation. After joining the softball team, I immediately knew three or four of these guys on the team would be lifelong friends. One friend in particular, Ethan, immediately took residence in my heart and would become one of the most inspiring people I have ever met, not to mention one of the funniest and most caring. Ethan was twenty-nine years old when I met him, and he had already served five years. Ethan was sentenced to life with no possibility for parole, which, in my opinion, is unfair and cruel in most circumstances. I saw Ethan, and I saw a man who was hurting, who was frustrated, and was coping in unhealthy ways. To judge him would have been totally insensitive as I didn't know how waking up every day with his type of prison sentence would have affected me. I knew I spoke lots to him about God and Jesus and that he never wanted to hear it. He was mad at God; he was wondering how a good God would allow him to receive the sentence he got. How God could take away a chance at a future, and how God could remove hope. I knew the verse Jeremiah 29:11 quite well. It was my life verse and had been since learning it. It says, "I know the plans I have for you, says the Lord, plans for a future and a hope, not for calamity."

I tried to convey that to Ethan, without being trite and insensitive. I remember how I felt when Craig told me Romans 8:28 while getting on the bus, and I didn't want to recreate that feeling for Ethan. I also remembered Craig had taught me we don't live based on feelings. We live focused on the truth, and the truth is God loves Ethan, and Jeremiah 29:11 is true for him as well.

My heart bled for Ethan, and I kept praying for him, sharing Jesus with him and letting him know there is a place he can go to lay those feelings and burdens down—the Cross. I did this daily for over three years, many times without him even being aware. Praying for him, praying with others about him, asking Craig, Jameson, and Trent to come in agreement with these prayers, it was a top priority. There were times when Ethan told me to knock it off, but I always came back. I chose to lead with love and meet him where he was at. Later, in my time at FSP, I began a job that had me working closely with Ethan daily. I would go to his desk, pray over him, often to myself as he did not like this much. I got in the habit of drawing Crosses on his desk, his notebooks, his working files, all while I prayed, which he chose to scribble out each time while telling me to knock it off and that he loved me, but he didn't want to see the Cross or hear about God. I was OK with this. I told him, "You can't make me not love you, Ethan, I am always going to."

My praying over him got to the point where he would not even stand there if I began, so I would often just lay my hand on his head or shoulder, which was normal for us when we talked, but I wouldn't talk. Instead, I would pray silently. He would look at me after a few seconds of not talking and ask, "What are you doing? You're praying, huh?"

My reply to this was to shush him and keep praying. Sometimes he laughed, sometimes he left, and sometimes he stayed and let it happen, all glory to God for his heart being changed, even if slowly. I even went as far as to hacking into his computer and setting up a reminder to pop up every day at 8:30 a.m. that said, "Luke loves you, and so does God. He loves you so much that He gave Jesus for you to be able to spend eternity with Him."

This showed up every day on his computer until the furniture shop closed in 2022.

God doesn't waste a thing.

# 30

Throughout my years living with Ethan at Folsom, I witnessed him treat people with love. I saw him rally behind the lonely person while championing the underdog on the yard and including them as much as he could. He spent lots of time and money training his mind and body in health and CrossFit so he could implement that knowledge to benefit those who needed it around the facility. He has such a huge heart, and he would spend so much effort caring about others. I would often point out to him he was living the life of a Christian by loving others and putting himself behind them. Yet he was choosing to not experience the love of Christ for himself by not believing in the One who is giving him that compassionate and loving heart. Ethan responded to that with "I will never give my life to the Lord," which always made me smile as my buddy Trent always pointed out what God chooses to do when people say never: He continues his redemptive powers in the "impossible situation," which will bring Him the most glory.

I continued to stay in contact with Ethan once I got released, and I stayed as diligent and consistent as ever in praying for him and sending him scriptures to read. I would even hide prayers in the middle of my letters to him so he would read the prayers as he was making his way through my letters from the streets updating him on what I was up to. I loved getting calls and letters from Ethan. He was one of my best friends inside of DOC and will always be one of my best friends, regardless of our addresses. I was confused one day when I got a call from Ethan, and he began our chat by telling me he got a new number. This made no sense to me as he doesn't have a phone number, and you will never change your DOC number, so I ask what he is talking about. Ethan says his number is 03052021, which still left me confused, until he told me it was the date of when he gave his life to the Lord and became a believer in Christ. Hallelujah! Amen! I am so honored to celebrate in his conversion and decision and give all glory to God. I am thankful for the encouragement God gave me to keep praying and to keep drawing the Cross on his desk. It was not a pointless act. God will redeem anyone, anytime, anyplace, no matter how long it takes them to see Jesus in their life. This single decision in Ethan's life might be at the top of the greatest blessings I have witnessed, and I still believe there is still much more to be written in his story as I am standing on the truth that God will break every chain binding us. I don't know how He will do it or when, but I believe God will deliver Ethan from his prison sentence on His timing.

God doesn't waste a thing.

# 31

It was during my time at FSP when my nephews and I really began to grow together and rebuild the relationships I destroyed by my actions. I owe a huge thank you to my brother Lee and his wife as they never allowed me to lose contact with their boys. They always supported the relationship and made it possible for me to write letters, send DVDs of me reading books to them, send pictures, as well as the increasingly important phone calls. We would speak multiple times a week, with many of the conversations being centered on God, the way He is working in our lives and how much He loves us. We would pray together, and this has become a constant in our day-to-day lives.

One of the reasons I am thankful for my time in prison is this beautiful relationship and how it is infinitely better than it was before I got locked up. Before prison, I was too selfish to think about my nephews, let alone focus on them, and I was too busy attacking my own agenda to devote any time, energy, or effort into their lives. Telling my nephews about my prison sentence was one of the most difficult conversations I and my family have ever had to do. But it has allowed for me to have a much more meaningful and joyful relationship with them, centered on Christ and His love for us.

God doesn't waste a thing.

CHAPTER
_____

# 32

Another great blessing God set in motion was yet another one that was greater than anything I could have ever asked for or imagined (Ephesians 3:20). Folsom was looking to bring another chaplain into the facility as one of their older chaplains was looking to come in less often because of health issues. Who did God put in place to fill this need? My great friend Trent! It was God's perfect timing that Trent was completing his apprenticeship the same month FSP was losing a chaplain and a position needing to be filled. This is when people who do not have a relationship with the Lord would utter one of my least favorite words, "coincidence," when it is not that. It is God and His great providence being worked out in our lives. It was truly awesome to reunite with Trent and once again spend time with him. He and I worked out our scheduling to where we could meet every Wednesday for a couple of hours and fellowship. It wasn't the time I had with him at SQSP, but those hours were vital in my continued growth as a believer and in my efforts to disciple others at FSP. Tough topics were brought up, honest discussions were had, and tears were shed. As we prayed, I realized more clearly God's plan for me and how to better help those in my circle of influence as I stepped into the arena of living with Jesus as my Lord and aligning according to His will in my life. I began to grow in my faith through these Wednesday sessions as I was seeing things with what I call "God goggles." I began to help others get to know Christ while trusting that God had a divine plan for my life. I still had my struggles, my doubts, and certainly some concerns, but they were far less often, and I didn't dwell on them nearly as long. And for those times when I needed some extra spiritual support, Trent was available. God knew who I needed and when I would need him, while also recognizing I needed time with less support so I could truly learn to lean on Jesus for my strength, my confidence, but most importantly, my identity.

God doesn't waste a thing.

# 33

R oughly a year into my time at Folsom, I began to inquire about getting into treatment for my crime. I was seeking the help in dealing with my past and my distortions while building on the responsibility and ownership I've taken for my actions. I had heard for years you cannot get out of prison without completing treatment, and it was nearly impossible to even get accepted into the program, let alone before my parole eligibility date (PED).

Here's a quick side note to help with some of the dialogue and context of what I will describe regarding sex offense sentences in California and how it affects the release of someone from prison, along with getting placed in treatment. There are two types of sentences: one is a determinate sentence known as a mandatory release date (MRD), which means there is a set date the state must let someone out by. Someone with that type of sentence is eligible to be released earlier than that date. They just cannot be incarcerated past that MRD; they get released no matter what. In my case, I received a twenty-year sentence with an MRD of November 2033, meaning California must release me on or before that date. The second sentence is known as an indeterminate life sentence, where someone has a date when they are eligible to be released after a minimum number of years, but they are never guaranteed release—they could be incarcerated for the rest of their lives. The parole board could essentially deny granting them parole for the remainder of their lives. An example of this type of situation was a friend of mine who received a five-year-to-life indeterminate sentence, where he was eligible for parole after three years. The parole board denied him for fourteen straight years until they decided it was time, after serving seventeen years. This is the type of sentence most of the men with a sex offense receive in California.

Knowing I had the MRD, I recognized through figuring out my earned time, which was ten days for every month served, I was able to determine when I would be eligible for release through parole by figuring out my PED. I used to ask Chaplain Craig when he thought I would get released, and he would tell me every time, without fail, "Not a day later than God wants you out."

And after years of that answer, I began to believe it. I also knew God would want me to be faithful in putting the effort on what I could control. The first thing I could control was figuring out who I needed to reach out to in DOC as far as getting into treatment. It turned out Folsom was the main prison in California, out of the thirty-five prisons they had at the time, that offered the Sex Offense Treatment and Management Program (SOTMP).

Thanks be to God. I fought going to San Quentin in 2014, when I begged to go to Kern Valley for protective custody until 2033, where He saved my life as that move led me to Christ. I also did not want to leave SQSP to come to Folsom, not knowing it was the prison I needed to be at to get into SOTMP and ultimately get released. Once again, God knew best and moved only as He could. Often God moves the mountain out of the way of the man, and other times He moves the man to the mountain.

God doesn't waste a thing.

# 34

Once I figured out I needed to meet with the mental health department at FSP, I sent kite after kite to the powers that be, asking for a meeting to know when I would be getting into treatment or even to be told what number I was on the waiting list. I found out the waitlist for SOTMP had thousands of people on it, upward of five thousand, and the list was being added to every day. I also learned there were only 148 spots available at a time, and it took roughly eighteen months for someone to complete the program and that there was about forty who finished a year. Most often I would get back a letter saying I was not even eligible to be placed on the waitlist as a person must be within four years of their PED to be added, which for me was still a year away. This was very depressing to know that if I were even added to the list, it could take decades to get my name chosen for the treatment. I wasn't thinking I would end up doing my whole twenty-year sentence at this point, but I didn't see how it would end up any differently. I kept repeating this process of sending kites, praying over them, and waiting for a reply, which rarely came. During this time, my normal day-to-day activities included working, playing sports, and going to services with a focus on showing Jesus to those around me as I led with love.

My time at Folsom continued to go well. I was making great friends, writing for the newsletter we created called *Pens & Perspectives*. I could share God while promoting love and hope to the men and staff at FSP. I also began helping in the pre-release program as the teacher of that class knew me from SQSP. He asked if I would be willing to come in and assist him in a few areas, specifically if I could help those who were close to leaving in creating resumes and running them through practice interviews to best prepare them for life in society. Both were skills I acquired while working in San Francisco as an executive recruiter prior to being incarcerated. This opportunity was lots of fun, and I got to see the men grow in confidence as they were approaching their release date. It was one of the best experiences I had, and I was thankful God allowed me to not only gain those skills in my past, but also create the opportunity to pass them along to those who needed it most.

God doesn't waste a thing.

CHAPTER

# 35

A quick glance into the financials of being in prison is that on average, most men earn $0.87 a day, which equals about $16 a month. After the state takes 20 percent for fines, fees, and restitution, a person is left with roughly $12.50 a month. From this, we would buy deodorant, shampoo, phone time, stamps, oatmeal, socks, etc., which is nearly impossible to do without the help of support sending in money from the streets. During my time in the chapel at SQSP, and while working in the library and pre-release at FSP, this is what I earned each month. December 2017, I was asked to work in the furniture shop, which was the correctional industry that built all the desks, cabinets, tables, and bookcases for the state of California. I was asked to be the director of sales. I took the job and was able to work closely with lots of great people: men who were in prison, people from the state department, other prison officials, as well as many universities and businesses in the community.

This sales role had me working daily with three of my best friends, Ethan, who I explained much of our work interactions earlier, as well as Brenton and Sammy. All of us had positions significant for the shop to be run successfully. This required the three of us to collaborate daily if the shop was going to be successful. When I took this job, I went from making $12.50 a month to being one of the highest-paid inmates in DOC, with an average monthly paycheck of around $245. This allowed me to save some money for my hopeful release. I was also able to increase my tithing to those who were not as blessed as I was in the facility.

God doesn't waste a thing.

# 36

There is a funny story I need to share of how Brenton and I got connected and became such close friends. It took place on the basketball court, with us playing pickup games one evening for the entire gym time. I didn't really know Brenton at the time. I was aware of him and knew he was a young, enthusiastic, athletic guy who loved hoops, working out, and that he worked in the furniture shop. I also knew Brenton was affiliated with the Bloods as he had been a gang member for over half of his life, but that was the extent of our relationship with each other. Brenton has one of those contagious personalities, and I felt God calling me to get to know him. At the time of this night, when we played basketball, he was working in the shipping department of the furniture shop, where he cleaned product and got it wrapped in cellophane so it could safely travel to the customer. Every time I saw him at the shop for the rest of that week, which was multiple times a day as he worked by Sammy and Ethan, I would act like I had the most horrific blister from basketball, which was causing a horrendous limp. One of the things I always tried to do in DOC was lighten the mood and bring joy to people through laughter as a laugh can transform an atmosphere, and prison is one that needs transformed mightily. This simple act of limping and whining about a blister cracked Brenton up each time. As I later learned about Brenton, he not only has a great sense of humor, but he is also one of the funniest guys around in any group, along with being ridiculously smart. There is much more to share about Brenton and the ways God used in him in DOC and the miracles he experienced. But I must say, had it not been for that blister, I am not sure if he and I would have become friends. As a matter of fact, nobody would have ever thought a young black gangbanger and an older white sex offender would have become buddies, let alone the best of friends.

God doesn't waste a thing.

# 37

A fter that week of limping, I began to go by Brenton's room in Cell House 8 to just see what he was up to. He then began coming by my room after dinner as there were usually five to six guys crammed in there, hanging out each night. Soon enough, Brenton had become a staple in not just the room hangouts, but in our overall group as well. I also think he was a fan of the trail mix I made using different candies, nuts, and seeds I got off the canteen each week. Getting more time with Brenton to chat, hang out, and discuss God, I got to learn what really made him tick and just how much he loves his kids and wants to follow God's will for his life. He just didn't understand yet how to accomplish that. A specific blessing came into his life shortly after he and I spoke about him not wanting to work in shipping anymore, rather him wanting more of a challenge and responsibility in the shop. We prayed about it and discussed him focusing on being faithful in the little things, and within two weeks of that prayer, Brenton was done wrapping product as he got hired in the office working at the desk right beside me. Brenton was promoted to the furniture shop's human resource director, where he handled all the administrative processes as well as attendance and payroll. Two years later, when I found out I was getting released, I trained him to take over the sales position. His ability and promotions in the shop remind me God will not let talent and heart go unused. God doesn't always use the qualified, He qualifies the ones He wants to use, and God certainly wanted to use Brenton at FSP.

Throughout my three years of hanging out with Brenton, nearly every hour of every day, I saw much growth and maturity as he continued to press into Jesus and walk trusting God had a divine plan for his future. Brenton became a member of *Pens & Perspectives*. He immediately took ownership and responsibility for creating excitement and buzz to the newsletter in ways we had not thought of doing yet.

Regarding *Pens & Perspectives*, it might be essential to point out what we were creating each month was beginning to get noticed by more than the people who were at Folsom. We eventually got approached by Stanford University (SU) and their Prison Arts Agenda (PAA) group to create a statewide newspaper. The intention behind the newspaper would be to highlight all the inmates and their families while creating a space for all to share what it is they were going through their incarceration story and situation. When we first heard of this possibility, I remember sharing with the group that I think a goal should always be to give a voice to the voiceless while creating hope for the hopeless. This opportunity with SU-PAA was a huge deal. Not only did it come with the support of one of the finest universities in the country, but it also garnered the support of the DOC Director of Prisons Jess Dean. Mr. Dean, a huge advocate for growth and creating normalcy inside of the prison walls, also brought in the support of the highest office in California—the Office of the Governor. All this created an opportunity for lots of good to take place and for all of us to step into our gifts and callings as we began to create a statewide prison newspaper that gave a voice to all thirty-five facilities in California. God began putting this in place long before any of us knew what was about to happen, but He certainly didn't waste our efforts on *Pens & Perspectives* or even the tiny newsletter back at SQSP in 2014 that got this ball rolling.

God doesn't waste a thing.

# 38

During our time creating the newspaper *The San Quentin News* (The SQ), we all had lots of opportunities to do something that could impact the future of incarceration in California for the better. One of the greatest moments for *The SQ* was when Brenton had the pleasure of interviewing Jess Dean, who, again, was the director of prisons in California. Brenton sat down with the most influential and powerful man in the state, regarding incarceration, other than the governor, of course. Brenton carried himself well and acted very professionally as he asked insightful questions in a confident manner that put Mr. Dean at ease and allowed for an invigorating and very educational conversation to take place. It quickly went from an interview into a relaxed conversation between two men. After that interview, I had the chance to chat with Mr. Dean briefly, where he and I discussed how I wanted to implement change and growth in prison and on parole when I got released. In a way only God can arrange, it was eighteen months later, when I was out in the community, when I got a call from the director of parole. He told me he was given my name from Jess and was encouraged to reach out and see if we could collaborate on instilling change in the parole system. I was later added to a task force that had a focus of rewriting and implementing regulations for offenders who were on parole in the state of California. There were state employees on this task force as well as parole officers, parole board members, even government officials, and me, a man who was currently on parole himself, rewriting the very rules he was following in the community. God did not let the moment pass inside of Folsom when Mr. Dean came in for an interview, when He knew I would later be needed in the community to make changes within the task force. This ultimately led me to work with Mr. Dean and the DOC to implement a work release program for the men inside of the facilities.

God doesn't waste a thing.

CHAPTER

# 39

There was a certain miracle Brenton got to experience that I was blessed to have been a witness in seeing God's handiwork in his life. Brenton grew up in the gang life. He was a member of the Bloods and was very active in that world leading up to his imprisonment. Brenton came into the Department of Corrections in 2014 and immediately thrusted himself into the political scene of gangs inside the walls. Because of this, he got tagged as an active member of the Bloods and was placed on the Security Threat Group (STG) list, which is not a list anyone wants to be on. Being on the STG list is another way for the department to track an individual as well as discipline someone whenever they choose to do so. A detriment this label carries is anything considered to be negative or dangerous in the eyes of the prison administration can, and often does, get anyone who is on the STG list for the specific gang involved in the situation locked down. When this happens, the person locked down loses privileges and freedoms, even if it has nothing to do with the gang or the person specifically. This was happening to Brenton often, especially the part of him getting locked down when a situation had nothing to do with him. Another disadvantage of the list is it can keep a person out of programs to help the man grow or gain education, while it also sets a rule that the person, Brenton in this case, can't easily progress to a custody level lower than medium. This hurts when it comes time to put in for parole or getting granted the chance to progress into community.

For the first year of Brenton's time in prison, he did some things he would say were not wise, very harmful, and certainly not his best moments. He would explain this is what happens to many of the young men who come into prison either already in a gang or ones that get recruited once they get sentenced and land on their prison yard looking for family, security, and an identity. This often leads to loss of earned time, potential days spent in the hole, and the inherent possibility of new charges added to your sentence.

Thanks be to God, Brenton made a mature and somewhat dangerous decision—to walk away from the gang to commit his life and future solely to God by following Jesus. This was considered dangerous because gangs do not allow members to just quit the gang, not without a severe and brutal price to pay. The gang themselves will turn on the one who is trying to leave and create some extremely violent situations and outcomes, which is where the phrase "blood in, blood out" came from. Blood is needed to be shed for initiation into the gang, and one can only leave the gang with bloodshed as well, often from death. This, however, was not the case for Brenton. The way Brenton carried himself, his level of honesty to the gang, and his commitment to his faith allowed for this separation from the Bloods to be a smooth one and certainly an uncommon one.

Regarding the gang, Brenton was no longer an active member of the Bloods, but in the eyes of the DOC, he absolutely was. They don't see many men make this decision, so they don't usually take anyone off the STG list. Brenton wrote to the prison administrators, as well as to the gang coordinator, and informed them all he was no longer a member of the gang. He told them the truth and shared with them he has become a Christian and is living a life focused on listening to the Holy Spirit and being guided as such. He finished the letter requesting they investigate his file and see his involvement with the church, *The San Quentin*, CrossFit, and his work evaluations in a trusted position at the furniture shop to show he has made changes in all areas of his life. This letter was returned to him basically saying they are not going to remove him from the list, that they hear this story all the time. This news was frustrating for Brenton and many of us who were friends with him as we had seen the growth and change in his life. But he did not let it deter him from living a life chasing Jesus. For the next couple of years, Brenton continued to help others while maintaining great relationships with those around him and keeping a positive outlook on his future. I was very proud of him for this, and many men at Folsom were blessed by how he was living his life.

One afternoon, as Brenton and I were working out on the weight pile, there was an announcement over the loudspeakers throughout the entire prison calling for Brenton to go to the Administration Offices. This type of call, to that specific office, is not normally a good thing. Brenton got the attention of Sergeant Stenson to let him out of the "pile," and he got escorted up to the gang coordinator's office. I was nervous and very curious as to what this could be. I spend most of every day with him, and I knew he had not done anything to get in trouble. I began praying for God to go before him and fill that office with His presence. Brenton came back about thirty minutes later, smiling, and told me he was no longer on the STG list. I began laughing and told him, "Well, that is a huge blessing. How did that happen?"

He shared with me that the gang coordinator told him they had been monitoring him and watching how he had been living the past fifteen to eighteen months, in person and on camera, and they realized he couldn't possibly be an active member of the Bloods.

I, of course, asked for more clarification, to which he said, "I had to as well."

They told him, whenever they checked to see what he was doing on the yard, in the cell house, or at work, he was doing it with me, a white guy who is a sex offender; Sammy, a white sex offender; Ethan, a white guy, who is in for murder; and another friend who was white, a sex offender, and gay. They told him there is no way the Bloods would allow a member of their gang to associate so much with that many white guys, who happened to be sex offenders, with one being gay as well. For that reason, they told him they are removing him from the list. This journey with Christ is so cool when you begin to see Him work miracles in the lives of your friends and those around you. God can do anything to further His kingdom and accomplish His will, and He will use anyone to do so, including a handful of white guys, several sex offenders, and one gay friend.

God doesn't waste a thing.

# 40

One day, while I was working in the furniture shop, standing at my desk with Brenton sitting at his desk just to the left of mine, I had a moment that was years in the making. I was about to come face-to-face with one of the first miracles in this journey I am on, which will shed some light not just on my DOC time to this point, but also how amazing God is in creating paths for His kids. Out of the corner of my eye, I see a man, dressed nicely in a suit and tie, step into our office. As this happens, I don't do a double take—I do a triple take—and then find myself trying not to hug this man as I lead with my hand for a handshake. Brenton, at this point, has a puzzled look on his face as visitors or other DOC staff come into the office daily, and this is not a normal reaction for me. Well, this is not a normal man, this is one of my heroes, and I still haven't even heard the whole story behind his helpful actions. As we shake hands, I say, "Paul, what are you doing here?"

He replies, "I'm the new fire and safety officer here at FSP." Then he followed it up with, "How is your dad, Jack, doing?"

My jaw dropped. I was speechless and about to cry as I realized he cared for me and my family then at Mule Creek, and he still does. I quickly told him my pops is good and that it's great to see him. I also thank him for what he did for all of us in 2014.

Paul acknowledged my gratitude and asked if I would like to hear about the whole situation and get the specific details. Excitedly, I step into my boss's office and told him, "Get out, we need your office."

With a smile, he fired back, "You don't tell me what to do, and I already know all about the details at Mule Creek," as Paul had checked up on me in the past.

This comment from my boss spoke to the heart and to the love God had placed in Paul for a moment just like this. My boss stayed, and I shut the door as we all settled in to hear about the scariest moment of my life. What follows next is a summary of the story as told to me by Paul.

"Luke, as soon as your face appeared on the news, the staff at Mule Creek, officers, and case managers began to hear that there was going to be attacks and violence directed at you. That is why you got pulled from working in the kitchen. They didn't want you in there with less staff and the kitchen knives. However, as the next couple of days went on, and you were being followed by several gang members, the threats became more serious. To this point, I still have not been made aware of your situation as I hadn't been working at the facility those days, and I wasn't supposed to be there the day that I pulled you from your room, but my daughter had car problems, which led me to working at Mule Creek that week."

God doesn't waste a car problem!

He continues, "I get into work the day that I eventually make the decision to pull you, and I learn that your dad has called the facility many times and is told by other officers that they do not care if there is a threat on you, that is part of prison. I am also made aware that there have been several offenders from the pod that you were living in, telling staff that there was a plan to kill you, and there has now been a 'green light' placed on you, allowing anybody from any gang to be able to kill you with no consequences. After hearing this, the staff responded to the offenders that it wasn't a big deal, and there are many other sex offenders left after you. It's at this time I catch wind of this warning as an offender comes by my office and tells me what is going on, where it is going to happen, when it will happen, and who is involved. I also hear that your dad has been calling in, trying to get someone to do anything to make sure that you are safe, but could not get much help, so I asked the next time your dad called in for it to be sent to me. I got your dad on the phone and gave him a rundown of what I knew and what I was planning on doing."

At this point of listening, I am so thankful to Paul and that I have the father that I have. He never, ever, quit showing up for me. Ever.

"Luke, it is here when I made the decision to send in the Special Operations Response Team (SORT) to get you and bring you to my office. When you got here to me, I was able to give you a bit of an explanation of what was going on, but not all of this."

Paul asks me if I would like him to continue as he can see tears in my eyes as well as the eyes of my boss. I tell him yes, and he continues.

"The specifics were that you were going to be followed to chow by a couple of the guys in the gang, and when you got through the first gate, they were going to shut that gate behind you, as well as the gate in front of you, that goes to the chow hall. This stretch of gates is an area that has few cameras leading up to it and none in between the two. Once they had you locked in between the two gates, you were going to get attacked, and they said you weren't going to leave unless in a body bag or on a stretcher. I knew I didn't have much time to intervene as your unit was getting called to chow in less than an hour."

As I heard this, I am overwhelmed with emotions, scared about what could have happened, angry that the first officers didn't do anything, thankful that Paul made the decision he did, and reminded why my dad is my hero. I asked if they caught who was going to do this, and he told me they did and found them with shanks on their bodies.

We finished chatting. I got up, thanked him for sharing this with me now and for saving my life. I shook his hand and headed back to work. It's at this moment I more clearly saw how God was working back then at Mule Creek, even when I wasn't a believer, and how He was with me through my time at WSP, San Quentin, and still here at Folsom. From that conversation on, I never missed a chance to tell Paul how grateful I was for him as I saw him weekly throughout my time at Folsom.

My friends came to know who he was and what he did for me, and a couple of times, I heard Brenton and Ethan thanking him. This was such a wonderful moment for me because I was able to see that without Paul making his decision in 2014, Ethan and Brenton may not have been at the stage of life they were at. I was beginning to understand more clearly God and His supreme grace and perfect timing with each of these encounters. This ultimately made it easier for me to trust in God and His plan when I was faced with difficult situations. And trust me, they still came, but I knew Romans 8:28 was still true. It was true then, and it is true now.

God doesn't waste a thing.

# 41

One evening, when I was working out with Brenton on the weight pile, I had a moment where I felt the Holy Spirit moving inside of me to go do a very specific thing. That thing was very scary and uncomfortable, and I wanted nothing to do with it, which is how I knew it was from God and not my own idea. I felt and heard God compelling me to go speak to a specific man working out on the weight pile about forty feet from me about God. This was so significant because this man was one of the top guys in the gang I had my problems with and one of the men who gave the order for me to be killed back at Mule Creek in 2014. Not only was I going to talk about God to a member of the gang who tried to kill me, but he was also with six other members of the gang. Alex is this man's name. This was not how I wanted to spend my workout and certainly not whom I would have chosen to discuss Jesus with, so I ignored the feeling and went back to spotting Brenton on his next set. Well, that didn't last long as the next time I lay down on the bench, I felt the Spirit move again. Knowing God's will is greater than mine, and I've made a commitment to follow God rather than settle into what is comfortable, I chose to act. I racked my weights while praying for discernment, and I invited my angel to accompany me in this moment as I began to walk over to their area. Brenton stopped me and asked what I was doing. I told him I felt like I was supposed to go talk to Alex. He asked me what about, and I replied hesitantly, "I think God?" I had little confidence in my voice or myself.

This reply is met with Brenton reminding me of a few reasons why this was a terrible idea. "First off, Luke, those guys over there do not like sex offenders, which you are. They also don't like Christians—you're that too. And oh yeah, let's not forget, they tried to kill you, Alex specifically! Please don't go over there."

I understood all his points. I even agreed wholeheartedly with all his points. I still felt the Spirit leading me over there, so I told him, "I gotta go, bro."

He leaned back on the fence nervously watching, along with the rest of the men on the pile working out. I remember Craig told me if I was unsure if what I was doing aligned with God's will, to pray for the door of the opportunity to be closed, thus making it impossible to follow the feeling. I walked so slowly over there, trying to give God time to answer my prayer for a hurricane, tornado, even a riot to begin on the yard, forcing us to be locked down immediately. Nope, none of those things happened, and next thing I know, I am standing in front of Alex and his six buddies getting called names that reference me being a sex offender. It's weird because at this point, I am slightly nervous and not so much about how he will respond to me sharing Jesus. Honestly, I was more apprehensive about him hearing about Jesus from a sex offender and how he will react to that piece; my guess was a punch to the face. What took place next was 100 percent anointed by God. To begin with, I told him I was sorry to bother him, then I asked him in front of his buddies, if he would be willing to chat with me after his workout. He responded with the obvious follow-up question, "About what?"

I took a second and replied, "God." Then I turned my cheek, expecting this would be the time I got punched.

Alex had a puzzled look on his face for a moment as his buddies began to laugh and make fun of me for this conversation. That was until Alex responded, "Sure, when I am done working out."

Then it was his friends' faces that looked puzzled. I didn't wait around for another second. I got the answer to the question I had felt inspired to ask, and I hustled back to Brenton and the bench to finish our workout. As I lay down on the bench, I found myself thanking God for three specific things. One, that He provided me with the courage to step into the uncomfortable and ask the question. Two, that He went with me and covered me with His protection. And three, that He prepared Alex's heart to receive the question and reply yes. Roughly twenty minutes later, the rec officer unlocked the door to the pile. I told Brenton goodbye and that I had a conversation with Alex to get to. I walked out of the weight pile and waited. Shortly after, Alex sat down by me, and we began to talk. During the discussion, I shared with him my crime and explained a bit more about how the death threat had affected me and the route it put me on through DOC. He asked me to elaborate on why I felt the need to talk to him about God, which allowed me to explain my relationship with God, Jesus, and listening to the Holy Spirit. He shared with me his past and how the gang believed in attacking Christianity but how lately he had been interested in learning more about who Jesus is. Thank you, God, for once again having impeccable timing.

During this conversation, several times he had to tell his friends to leave us alone and to give us some space. It was awesome. Here I was, sitting with someone who tried to kill me, talking about God, and the gang is the thing getting "written off." God, you really do prepare a table for me in front of my enemies while protecting me and moving in their hearts. When it was time for yard to close, and we had to go in and lockdown, I prayed for the both of us and began to walk in. By the time we had gotten up the fifty-yard ramp into the unit, he had asked me if I would be willing to come back out the next night and continue the discussion. Enthusiastically, I said, "Absolutely!" and mentioned I would see him tomorrow. We hugged and went our separate ways.

The next night we were back working out when he came over and began asking questions about people in the Bible. We spoke for over an hour about God, Jesus, and my other favorite person in the Bible, Joseph. While talking about Joseph and how his brothers had planned on killing him, I could sense Alex was having an emotional reaction to this part of the story. He told me he was sorry for what happened to me at Mule Creek. I accepted his apology and told him I forgave him. From that day on, he and I were closer, not best friends, but we got along. I even got him to submit an article for *Pens & Perspectives*, where he chose to write about hope. Once again, God did not squander this opportunity to reconcile a seemingly irreconcilable situation.

God doesn't waste a thing.

# 42

Here's an update to the Alex conversation. It was July 2021, and I had been writing this very book you are reading, when I felt the Holy Spirit once again guiding me to Alex. I prayed about it and felt led to write and encourage him while also sharing how powerful that first interaction on the weight pile was for me in trusting and following the Spirit. I also needed to ask his permission to use his name in this book. A couple of weeks later, I get back the following letter from him.

September 9th, 2021

Luke,

Boy was I excited to read your mail. As irony would have it, I tell our story a lot! I've wanted so badly to contact you, a few days prior to receiving your letter I asked (name omitted) to see if we could find you. No luck. God is good though, out of the blue I get some mail from the worst 2nd baseman at Folsom, lol.

Seriously I'm stoked to hear from you, even more so to hear that you are doing well. Thank God for your redemption/second chance. As I give my testimony, your name is one I bring up as a farmer for Jesus. All these seeds you've planted, along with others truly helped me find my way home. In 2019 I gave my life to God. After leaving Folsom I went to High Desert State Prison and then Calipatria where I met Howard, Monty, Jacob, Bryan and Ryder (last names omitted). All, like you, helped me find God more so than ever. Over there I helped run Bible studies, as I grew in Christ. Helped run CrossFit, also a few other cognitive classes, 7-Habits, and such. Warden L. asked me to help run CrossFit here at Avenal State Prison, so I prayed and found my way here. Soon we will be taking our Level 1 Certification Test at Folsom. Hopefully I pass. I am a bit nervous, but God willing I'll do fine.

I went to and from court a few times, no luck but one thing I realized coming back from this was, I need God's help. We can never just do things on our own. I never truly understood that until I felt and heard God speak to me. Then I knew I needed God in my life. Mid 2020 I filed a waiver for my clemency, 6 months later, February 2021 I got accepted to file 4 years early! Also, Fresno County started a new "Conviction Integrity Unit." Basically, they look at inequity in sentencing, as well as harsh sentencing. Possibly I can be looking at a 16–48-year sentence, any of which I will be home if they resentence me. Nervous about that as well!!

Anyway, please write back, maybe you can give me your number, so we can talk. Keep up the good work and YES you can use my name anytime!

I love you bro, take care and always remember eyes up! Thank you for the support.

Sincerely,
Alex

The truth of how much God can change hearts has never been more noticeable than it has been in this situation. This man, who once signed off on me being killed and a list of others being hurt, is now leading Bible studies. Alex is now fighting for Jesus while being an example to others of how to choose God over gangs. He walked away from the gang and ran to the Cross. Alex gave his life to the Lord. He is now an inheritor to the Almighty King and a walking testimony for how God can transform a life.

God doesn't waste a thing.

CHAPTER

# 43

I t is during this time that FSP had made the decision to move the
incentive pod out of 6-Upper and send us down to Cell House 8. Their
goal was to create a combined incentive and industry workers unit to
have all of us in the same place in case of a lockdown in the facility, where
they could still use us in running the facility. This was not the most ideal
situation as Cell House 8 is much larger and louder, but at least all of us
friends were still together. We made the best out of this situation and chose to
look to the positives rather than dwell on the negatives we could not control.

As far as serving prison time, I would say things were going well. I had
lots of friends and was involved in sports, studies, and groups throughout the
facility. One thing was still bothering me, and it was that I was still seeking
help with getting into SOTMP. Not only was I not getting into treatment,
but I also couldn't even get a response from them. This silence created in
me a sense of helplessness, along with hopelessness. For months on end, I
would write weekly kites asking for help, never getting a reply. This led to
some obvious discouragement, which I was apparently carrying quite clearly
on my face the next time I got to see Chaplain Craig, when he came to FSP
to work a day with Trent, who was now a permanent chaplain at Folsom.

I left work early on this Wednesday as I normally did to go visit with

Trent. Only this time I stepped into the office and to my surprise, Craig was in there too. Normally, this would have been the only blessing, and it would have been enough of one, yet God had another outcome planned out. During our chat, I told Craig things were going well, and I was thankful I got moved here, but he must have sensed my discouragement. He asked me to be honest and get to what is bothering me so we can discuss it, pray about it, and get past it. I spoke to him about my frustration with the Mental Health Department, that I hadn't been able to get any response from them, and that I would like prayer for their hearts to soften and get back to me and for God to remove the angst and anxiety this situation was causing me. The three of us prayed and asked God to let His will be done in this situation and to give us clarity and wisdom in how to proceed and cope with the situation in front of us. When we finished praying, through our normal catching up, Craig asked if I knew a therapist named Ms. M who worked at FSP, to which I said no, and he told me he had worked with her at SQSP before she transferred to Folsom.

Craig got up, walked across the hallway, after asking where the Mental Health offices were, and as only God could orchestrate, walked in and went to the first office with an open door. This was the office of Ms. M, and she just happened to not have a client in her office at this time. This was a divine appointment created by our great God. Next thing Trent and I saw, while sitting in his office, was the door opened, and Craig was walking in with Ms. M who introduced herself and asked, "What can I do to help you?"

I spoke to her about my situation, my crime, and how I had been hoping to get into treatment. The goal was to get help so I could continue to learn about how I allowed myself to make such destructive, selfish, and assaultive choices. I filled her in on the consistency of my requests through the kite system and how I was beginning to feel like there was no hope. She sat there, listening to my concerns and feelings, then she did what I can only describe as a miracle. Ms. M asked if I would fill out one more kite she could take to her supervisor. Her supervisor turned out to be the head of SOTMP in DOC, and just getting a kite or any form of contact with him was difficult, but getting a message personally delivered to him from one of his own therapists was a miracle, a miracle that came about because of a past working relationship between Craig and Ms. M several years earlier.

God doesn't waste a thing.

# 44

A day later, literally less than twenty-four hours later, I get the SOTMP supervisor Mr. G showing up to my cell house to chat with me about this kite. As we stood there speaking, he asked me what my goal was and what I would like to get accomplished from this kite. I shared I have spent lots of time over the past four years of my life, much while being incarcerated at SQSP, diving into what is truly important to me and where I find my identity. I further explained that much of my studying and self-reflection was rooted to my faith and relationship with Jesus Christ. God must have worked on his heart, and quickly, he set up an appointment for me to come sit with him and see how treatment looked for me, timing-wise, regarding my eligibility. The day comes for the meeting, and I show up excited and prepared. I'm also very nervous as I'm fully aware it'll be about another year until I am eligible for the waitlist to get into treatment. The list DOC was going by must not have been of concern to God as He had a different plan for how my therapy would begin.

During the meeting, Mr. G tells me I was not eligible for treatment. Therefore, I was not even on the waiting list for him to give me an accurate timeline. I let him know I knew that but was eager to have this chance to possibly begin to figure out how I went from helping people to hurting them. I asked if he could ballpark for me when I might not just be on the list, but also at the top of it. He explained there were usually over five thousand people on the list at any time and that it's normal to get around forty people through a year. With that being the math he was using, he told me I would be at the top of the list in about 120 years.

Gulp.

As I listened to that number, I realized there was nothing I could do about it and chose to ignore it. I asked him if I could share my thoughts on my crime and my feelings around it, and we spoke for the rest of the hour about my feelings and what I had learned about myself up to that point. Mr. G must have noticed my sincerity, my vulnerability, and my level of transparency. He came up with the idea of us meeting every couple of Fridays, where he and I could go over my past and begin to dive into my distortions, without officially being in treatment. This is without question a God thing as it is wilder and greater than anything I could have hoped for, especially since Mr. G does not even carry any clients on his caseload. I would be his only one.

As with Joseph, found in Genesis 37–50, always being in God's favor, I felt the same way in my situation both present and now starting to look back through some of my DOC time. I remember sharing with Trent this outcome regarding the Friday meetings with Mr. G and him saying, while smiling, "Another win on God's scoreboard."

We had discussed that I was truly just hoping to get a response about my eligibility. For as many people who were happy about this opportunity I was blessed with, there were just as many who became angry, jealous, and ultimately, vindictive. Jealousy runs rampant inside of a prison, even within groups of friends. Instead of focusing on the negatives, I chose to be thankful for the blessing while continuing to show love and encouragement to those who were frustrated toward me while pointing to the One responsible and giving Him the glory.

Meeting with Mr. G monthly, often twice a month, I began digging into my past. I was journaling about everything, from my thoughts regarding my sexual past to fantasies I had, even to how prison is becoming part of my future goals. I credit the ability to do this, without much fear, to Jesus and how He didn't give me a spirit of timidity and how He had clearly expressed to me many times that I am not identified by my past, but rather who I choose to live my future for.

At this point of my DOC time, I was staying supremely busy. I was getting emotionally, physically, and mentally stronger each day, but where I was seeing the most growth was spiritually. I was becoming more keenly aware of the blessings being bestowed upon me on a nearly weekly basis. God was showing Himself to be faithful and was allowing me the ability to see my life from a different perspective. I began to step back and look at how my moves and transitions had been laid out, not in the way I had wanted, but how God knew would be best. When I finally took the twenty-thousand-foot view, as they say, I was brought to tears. I recognized I was protected and exactly where God needed me to be. It was at this very moment I realized I would still be sitting in protective custody until 2032 had I gotten my way, had I not been threatened by the gang at Mule Creek and placed in a hole where I grew a beard. Seeing this allowed me to step up more courageously in my daily walk and how I chose to love and share my life openly and fully transparent.

Around this time, I was blessed to be a part of a new program set to begin regarding CrossFit in Folsom. This program is Redemption CrossFit (RCF), and it was not just a blessing to me, but also to hundreds of men and counting throughout FSP. CrossFit came into our facility because of the hard work and collaboration of not just the DOC administration and offenders, but also the community support in and around San Francisco and Sacramento. The mission is to heal hearts and bodies through CrossFit for the men and women inside of the prison system. God is in the business of healing hearts and bringing community together, and this program helped facilitate those agendas. As great as this program was for the unity and community of FSP, it also created opportunities for men to step into their passions and giftings, and this was never more visible than in my buddy Ethan. Ethan was a man who truly was seeking opportunities to help others, and he is the one who is often found hanging out with the outcast, trying to help them feel included. In life, this attribute is rare. Inside of a prison, it is almost impossible to find. Yet there Ethan was, filling the gap for the meek of heart. This was part of God's great redemption story for Ethan and how he needed to walk through RCF with others to not only help show them their miracles, but also for him to see his very own miracle in the process.

Through RCF, the program was offering an opportunity for men to not just be coaches, but also to study and take the test to become CrossFit Level 1 (CFL1) certified coaches. This is the same requirement men and women need to be coaches in the community. This gave men a chance to get certified so that upon their release, they will be qualified to work and earn a salary as a CrossFit coach in any gym in the country. This certification came at a cost of $1,000, which is awfully expensive for people who earn between $15 and $20 a month inside of a prison. Not only was that a potential barrier for Ethan, but he also had the sentence of life in prison, with no option for parole, other than when God decides to let him out this with his next miracle. With that being his truth for the time being and knowing he may not ever make a single dollar back on that $1,000 investment, he didn't get discouraged or let his heart waver. Ethan wanted to help the men at Folsom get healthier, in mind and body, and felt motivated to lead others to be the best version of themselves they could be. God honors that type of heart, and He also owns the cattle on a thousand hills, and God provided an anonymous donation to pay for the cost of the certification. That alone was huge, yet God was not close to being done working in this situation. Ethan needed to take the tests for his CFL1, which were given at a completely different facility across the state of California, and the DOC did not like putting men with life sentences in transport any more than they had to for security reasons. This was not a logistical issue for God as Ethan, along with four other men, traveled across the state to High Desert State Prison to take their tests on two separate days. All five of them passed their tests, and all of them got their CFL1.

God doesn't waste a thing.

# 45

CrossFit became part of the normal daily activities for me and so many others at FSP. It was great. It led many men to finding their path to community and living a healthy life while being in DOC. Adding this into my routine was a true joy as I was working in the furniture shop, hanging out with some great friends, speaking to my nephews regularly on the phone, and meeting with Mr. G a couple of times a month to chat about my life. It was a smooth life, and as my dad always told me when I called home, "Smooth is boring, and boring in prison is a good thing!"

Well, life was about to get a new wrinkle added to it, by way of another article written about me in the media and stories about me on the news.

I was chatting with Brenton in my room when somebody popped their head in and asked me if I had seen the paper yet. I had not. I never looked at the paper. He tells me I am on the front page of the paper yet again. I cannot believe this. I can't fathom what I am hearing. It has now been about five years since my incarceration and three years since the last media blast at Mule Creek that led to a death threat. I was annoyed, and of course, it was not a comfortable feeling. However, things are different now. I am different now. My relationship with the Lord was different. It's present, it's deeper, and it was what I was identified by. Jesus gets to label who I am, not the man writing for some California newspaper. Surprisingly, I am calmer than I thought I would be. I'm still not happy about the extra attention I was getting, but I was certainly not panicked. What's even cooler is the events that followed. To begin with, I had at least eight friends pile into my room to support me and to remind me they loved me and had my back. Thanks, Ethan, Sammy, James, Hector, Sonny, Brenton, Clive, Tony, and Monty. It meant a lot to me. This encouragement was amazing, but that was just the beginning of the people coming by my room. I had the leader of the Bloods, the leader of the Crips, and even the leader of the gang that tried to kill me step into my room, together, to let me know I was safe and that nobody from any of their gangs were going to threaten or harm me. This article, they said, proved to them I was telling the truth while living at FSP and that they were proud of how I was handling all this. The dichotomy of the two separate "newspaper" events is so bizarre when I think about them. At one event, gang members ambushed my room, threatened me, and created a plan to kill me. This time, though, friends came to support me. I still ended up getting ambushed by the gangs, only this time they were coming to the room with love and support, not shanks. God is so good, so amazing. He would not let a moment where a paper reported on me, which could potentially harm me, be used to show His redemptive powers even through the likes of what could be considered "enemies."

God doesn't waste a thing.

# 46

If God had stopped there, it would have been one of the largest miracles I had seen as it is rare to get those three gangs to agree on anything, let alone the support of a sex offender in a prison, but that's not how my God works. There is more to this media incident and how it is going to impact my future in the Department of Corrections. I may have been reassured I was safe, and this felt great and added to the ease I had already felt in trusting in God. However, DOC is still a government agency, one that oversaw my safety for the time being. Looking just three years back into my file, they could see the last time I was brought up in the media, it was followed with death threats and an actual plan to be carried out, so it's not out of the question to think they would react the same by pulling me from general population and move me. This would have been the worst-case scenario in my opinion. I have got great friends and an awesome job. I am meeting with an SOTMP therapist about my past, and my buddy Trent is chaplain here. I don't want to go anywhere, but clearly, I have learned from before, this is not a decision I have the power to make.

After this news hit, I certainly had the feeling I was going to get called into the Warden's office or at least somebody in the administration department. That didn't happen. God had appointed a different type of meeting for me to experience. When I was at work in the furniture shop, I got called into my boss's office, the same one in the previous discussion with Paul. I would get called into his office five to ten times a day because of my role in the shop and how closely he and I needed to work together, so getting called in there was not alarming. This time was different though. He had me shut the door and take a seat while he turned his chair and looked at me, completely ignoring his computer and work. This meant we are not having a work chat; this was serious. He proceeded to tell me he had been made aware of my situation and that the administration had reached out to him to see if he knew anything, but that they were also looking into what they were going to do next to keep me safe. My boss, who was a major, was often brought into these situations for a couple of reasons. One, he had many years of experience on this side of DOC and gang situations, and two, but more importantly, he had hired most of the leaders of the different gangs on the yard in the furniture shop and had a good rapport with them and figuring out the temperature of most gang-related incidents.

He shared with me earlier he had someone from the Bloods, the Crips, and the "White Boys" come into his office, together, and they told him nothing was going to happen to me, whether at work, in the cell house, or on the yard. In his decades of working in this capacity, he had never seen a moment like this, especially for someone with my type of crime. He was amazed, and to be honest, I was too. I told him it's all God's provision and His protection. I thanked him for his time and began to get up to go tell Brenton of this news. He wasn't done yet though.

As I sat back down, he let me know he called the powers that be, so the administration team, and told them what had happened, that I am probably safer here than anywhere else, and to *not* move me from Folsom and to put me on the facility hold list. The facility hold list was a list where inmates could be placed to keep DOC from moving them to another facility. The reason for this list was that some prisoners were essentially too valuable to a facility and how it operated to let them leave. With much gratitude in my heart, I again thanked him. I got up, thank God, and never thought about moving again.

God doesn't waste a thing.

# 47

Up to this point, I had seen God move mountains and move me. I had also seen He had moved the hearts of men who used to breed hate, and now they emote love. He had used major tragedy to bring about immense glory, and He had found a way to make the worst situations become the best arenas to show Himself to be amazing and faithful. Here is a quick list of the things God had not let go to waste:

1. Threats from a gang within twenty-four hours of getting into DOC
2. An article and news report updating the community about my crime
3. Hatred from a gang with murder in their hearts
4. A daughter's car breaking down
5. A man with a heart for helping
6. A lady who loves big beards and math
7. An older chaplain who had patience while listening to ranting and raving
8. A young chaplain who loved me for who God sees me to be
9. A man who hadn't spoken for three years singing "Amazing Grace" for the heavens to hear

10. A friend's time in a hyperbaric chamber to allow for a meeting with angels
11. An atheist who eats metal living with a hole in his stomach
12. A jealous case manager who didn't like Christian relationships
13. An open chaplain position at Folsom
14. A story shared from a past friend five years later about a murder plan
15. A visit from the Holy Spirit during a workout to go speak with an old enemy
16. A reunion between a therapist and a chaplain
17. A passion for helping by a therapist
18. A second round of articles in the newspaper
19. Rival gangs rushing to support a child of God
20. DOC administration taking the advice of gangs at their facility

After having experienced all this in my past and seeing God and His faithfulness, up to this point, it was not out of the question to trust and believe He was not going to waste a second round of articles and media attention in His plan for my life.

# 48

Sitting down for my next meeting with Mr. G after being in the media was a bit of an overwhelming but blessed moment for sure. The thing was he did not even know I was in the paper. I kind of figured of all the people who would know, or should know, it would be the mental health department in charge of SOTMP, but nope. I began to explain how the last few days had been and the conversations I have had with people about this, and even the conversations others have had about me and on my behalf about this event. As this conversation was taking place, I noticed a few things were happening. First thing was that I was more calm and less emotional about it than I thought I would be. Glory to God for that. Second, I could see some wheels turning in Mr. G's head. At this point, I had just become eligible for treatment as I was now officially within four years of my PED. However, I was keenly aware of the thousands of people who were also on this list and that I had about 120 years until it was my turn.

This, as with most of the situations God worked in and through, was a huge obstacle in my path, one that looked immovable and impossible to cope with. Let me continue with what transpired next. Mr. G made a phone call to the powers that be at headquarters, and they began to dialogue with one another in a manner that was completely miraculous. Some of the things spoken about were how one of the greatest safety attributes most men in prison have going for them, especially someone with a sex offense, is the gift of perceived anonymity. Although most people may think they know the details of another man's crime, the fact is they often don't. Thinking, guessing, and speculating were totally different from seeing it on TV and reading about it in the paper. This creates much less doubt and conjecture as facts are typically what is attempted to be reported. When doubt is removed, it often generates a powder keg of violence and danger as I personally witnessed at California City and Mule Creek, as people in prison often join in on a mob mentality in times of hatred.

As the conversation continued, Mr. G pointed out I was no longer anonymous. Rather, I was the most visible and talked-about offender in the California Department of Corrections and that I had been meeting with him for about a year without even being in group, taking responsibility for my actions and my crime while discussing what distortions I had that allowed me to create a victim and, more importantly, how to prevent it from ever happening again.

I believe this related to God's promise: "If you are faithful in the little things, you will be afforded the ability to be faithful with the big things."

I took treatment seriously long before treatment took me seriously as a client. Toward the end of the discussion with DOC Headquarters, Mr. G was asked what he wanted to do with this situation, and he said he felt it would be best to use this momentum and the fact that I was in the media, as well as my level of intentionality with treatment, and place me in the program for treatment. When he hung up, he informed me I would be signing my treatment contract that day.

PRAISE GOD! Obstacle obliterated.

In a matter of minutes, I was moved from being on a 120-year-long waitlist to a group that day, all because of God and how He can use things intended to harm us to glorify Him.

God doesn't waste a thing.

# 49

A couple of days later, I got moved to Cell House 6-Upper again, which was a giant blessing to get back into those rooms and not have to sleep with my head right beside a toilet. I was also in the onboarding process for treatment when it struck me once again how perfect God and His timing was. Remembering back to when I described there were two different types of sentences men with sex offenses got— either an MRD, which again was what I got, or an indeterminate sentence, which brought with it the real possibility of never actually getting released from prison. There had long been chatter about a lawsuit claiming it was unfair to those with indeterminate sentences that they cannot get released without treatment, yet they often could not get treatment if a spot was taken up by someone with an MRD, who would be released, no matter what, when their discharge date came.

This chatter became law roughly two weeks after I signed my contract to begin treatment; this law stated that someone with an MRD would no longer be accepted into treatment as those spots were for those who have life sentences. This law, as with all laws, especially inside of prison, would probably be challenged and potentially reversed, but as it stood at the time, it meant that if God didn't plan all things for good, even the timing of a newspaper article, I may not have been able to get into treatment at all, leaving me doing my entire twenty-year sentence. I would not have been allowed to leave in 2020; rather, I would have had to sit inside of DOC until 2032. It is important to remember, back in 2014 at WSP, I begged for protective custody and with it a release date of 2032 anyways. Once again, I was grateful God had a greater plan and purpose than I could have ever imagined, and that it is not my will, but His will, that gets done.

God doesn't waste a thing.

CHAPTER

# 50

I had mentioned earlier we had begun the newspaper *The San Quentin*, and things were going well for the team. We had nailed down all the logistical items necessary in the beginning of a project of this magnitude. How often we would publish? Who would do the publishing? Where will we get it printed? Who would deliver them to the other prisons? That's just to name a few, and we were getting closer to putting together our first issue. It would not come out for a while as we still had to run it through the process for the first time, but we were putting the artwork and the articles together from the men and women who were incarcerated in California, along with the pieces sent in from their families that made this first cut. It was groundbreaking and exciting.

Personally, I had a goal for what I wanted to accomplish within this first issue, and it was to continue stepping out of my comfort zone to again face my fear in terms of sharing my crime with others inside of a prison. I trusted God had brought this to my heart again, so He must have a goal of His own that He wished to see come to fruition through *The San Quentin*. I chose to write an article about what it was like being a sex offender and what my SOTMP experience had been like. By this time, I was about to complete treatment. Through this article, I was hoping to claim ultimate victory over Satan and his lies of using my crime as a place to add anxiety and fear into my life by sharing that I am not identified by my crime, but by my God. This was exactly what I did, going against the counsel of friends, DOC staff and administration, even people in offices higher than I could imagine. I trusted in God and what was revealed to me by the Holy Spirit. I chose to move forward with the article.

Prior to the publication of issue 1, I got called into the administration office at Folsom and was told writing an article called "My Sex Offense Therapy Experience" may not be the wisest or safest move in prison. They stressed that just a few years earlier, there had been a death threat on my life because of a similar type of story about me and that this was about to get sent out to all thirty-five California facilities, not to mention parole, government officials, senators, and even governors in multiple states. I completely understood their argument but pointed out that my life was different now, and I was aware of the circumstances, but God was in control of this situation and the outcome. I proceeded with the publication, and I was 100 percent at ease in trusting that God had something planned through this article that was greater than me. Through my work in the chapel job and going through treatment, I had come to promise myself and others I would live honestly and be vulnerable in my growth. I chose to live intentionally in my interactions with others and how I followed the Holy Spirit. This situation was no different, and it wasn't about me.

God doesn't waste a thing.

CHAPTER

# 51

The issue came out in April 2020, and our whole team was excited. Stanford University was thrilled, as was the entire Department of Corrections team, from FSP to the director of prisons office, as well as the governor's office. With all this enthusiasm, I never lost sight of the article I wrote and my hope of it being as freeing for others as it was for me. Regarding the article specifically, I got lots of positive feedback toward it, yet one interaction stood out over the others. It was the early part of May 2020; I remember because I left May 27, and this happened close to when I would be getting reintegrated back into the community. I was walking alone in the recreation yard, working out and praying, trying to get my mind and body ready to leave prison, when I see a very large Native American man walking across the yard on a straight line to me. As he was approaching, he was also trying to get my attention, shouting, "Hey, hey you, newspaper guy!"

At this point, several thoughts crept into my mind, one being that I was probably the only newspaper guy out here, so he clearly had not mistaken me for someone else, and two, I was really hoping he wasn't coming up to fight me because of my article. Not only was I leaving in a little under a month and I don't want to mess that up by getting in trouble for fighting, but I also don't think I would have done very well in this fight if I am being honest; he was big. I prayed quickly and asked for God to be glorified in this encounter and to give me the strength to do what is right, not what is easy, and with that, he was right in front of me.

As he stood in front of me, I looked at him and asked, "What's up, bro?"

He smiled and asked if I was Luke, to which I said yes, and he followed it up by asking if I was the guy who wrote the article about being a sex offender. Again, I said yes and noticed that this man was beginning to tear up. He stood right in front of me, stuck out his hand, and said, "That's awesome. To have the guts to write about your past that way."

I thanked him and told him it was God who gave me the courage to be vulnerable. The next words that came out of his mouth broke my heart. He told me he was sentenced to DOC for a sex offense and that he had refused treatment for the past decade because he couldn't risk letting his gang know about his past. He also told me I was the first person he had shared this news with, ever, and that he wished he could share his past the way I was able to.

I asked him if he would be OK with me praying for him, as I felt led to pray, but did not want to disrespect him and his Native American beliefs. I remember, from my three years of setting up their services at San Quentin, that many do not like to engage in prayer with Christians. But not this man, he said sure. I prayed for him and for God to give him the courage to step into his future and to trust that there was an amazing plan for his life. We finished praying and went our separate ways.

As I finished my walk, for the remainder of that yard time, I found myself contemplating that this man had been suffering with emotional and spiritual bondage, much like I did for my first few years at SQSP. He didn't feel like he could be honest, and this refusal to be vulnerable was literally keeping him from his actual freedom from prison because he wouldn't get released until he completed treatment. It's the perfect picture of choosing to live a life of bondage because of fear and lies from the devil. It also shined a spotlight on God and His great redemptive powers. A few days before I left FSP, this same man told me he put in a kite to speak to SOTMP and that he told them he was ready to receive treatment.

God doesn't waste a thing.

CHAPTER

# 52

After completing treatment, I had the ability to do a few things that, God willing, would continue to promote health and safe reintegration for many incarcerated men in a similar situation as I was in. Once I finished my final project and shared it with my support on the streets, my group, my group therapists, and of course, my primary therapist, Mr. G, I was moved into the maintenance phase of the program. During this phase, I spoke with Mr. G about doing two things I felt would have a great impact on the program and moving it forward—helping the staff and the clients. First, I proposed creating a mentor program and utilizing the knowledge and support the men who were in maintenance had acquired to help other clients and relieve some work and stress off the therapists. Second, I brought up the curriculum that was being taught and how it was organized, implemented, and monitored. I did not think it was well organized and felt it was terribly written to be honest. I spoke with Mr. G and said I was very grateful I had the chance to go through the curriculum, but I felt it was difficult for others to follow and grow from it. After a few conversations, with him and the administration, he asked what I wanted to do about it, and I told him I wanted to completely revamp and reorganize the entire program, starting with the curriculum. Both requests, the mentor program and the overhaul of the SOTMP curriculum, were a long shot to get done as was even permission to attempt. Making change inside of a DOC facility must go through many steps and much red tape, and this is for a normal administrator, let alone a convicted felon who was in prison still. For many people and most involved in this process, this looked to be an impossible situation, but as I have seen in my past six years of prison, God loves to work in the arena of the impossible as once it gets accomplished, there was only One who could get the glory.

God doesn't waste a thing.

# 53

Regarding creating a mentor program, I was told to put together a few notes on what I wanted to create, why I wanted to do it, the benefits of the program, and logistically how it would work. Not only did I put all this together, but I also turned it into a proposal that addressed all their needs and potential issues as well.

**PROPOSAL**
**SOTMP MENTOR**
**PROGRAM**
SOTMP COORDINATOR – Mr. G
Proposed by Luke Chance

**Requirements:**

Completion of Track 1 of SOTMP

Finish in good standing with both group therapists and their primary therapist

Recommendation from a therapist and approval from a staffing of the Support Team

A job in the facility that understands the requirements of this new position

An ability to help when called upon throughout the day/night Living in Cell House 6-Upper: the SOTMP unit with access to all the pods/clients

Gives relevant feedback and explains the reasoning behind it

RMP was presented and clearly showing he has understanding on the project (RMP) and how to show not only the risks, but the knowledge gained and explains it well to others

### What a mentorship will entail, or look like:

Help with homework (Cycle, Brief Social History, Risks, protective Factors, RMP work, etc.)

Lead by example; will showcase how to utilize tools and skills learned in group

Be a good listener and have an ability to show empathy

Willingness to communicate to a variety of men, and their therapists

Motivate others in the program to challenge them to deal with the root of issues

Be flexible with their time and have an unselfish attitude to help others meet their goals

Demonstrate a positive attitude and act as a positive role model within the community

Values ongoing learning and growth in the treatment field

Provides honest and constructive feedback to inspire growth and change

Speak to Parole Officers or at special events about the program when needed

Will be available to go into groups who are in need of feedback or are struggling as a group

A mentorship is a highly valuable developmental activity, and one that will take a great program and turn it into an excellent program as it will allow for much more guidance and counseling from experienced participants. At the core of the program will be the relationship between the mentor(s) and the mentee(s), as the development of the mentee and his growth is the key focus. The relationship between the therapists and the mentor(s) is also paramount, as they will be the daily support for the therapists and will work alongside of them to help with any issues that arise.

### What the screening process will look like:

The mentor candidate will either be nominated by his group therapist, or he will ask for the opportunity to be a mentor. At this time the applicant will write a 1-2-page essay addressing:

Why they want to be a mentor?

What their purpose of a mentor is?

What are your strengths that will make you a good mentor?

There will also be an interview with the SOTMP coordinator to show competency of the material (ex: Cycles, High Risks, Triggers etc.) and if they can verbally explain and discuss the material. This will also allow for the coordinator to check compatibility with the team and see if it is a good fit based on personality/compatibility match. At this time the Treatment team can address specific questions or concerns with the applicant and choose to accept the applicant or not.

### Overview

Folsom State Prison will be the first facility to have available a mentorship team for the Sex Offense Treatment Program. This will make Track 1 more compatible and collaborative, much as it is in the community, where members of treatment are getting support from their peers. This mentoring will allow for those who have just finished group; and/or in Maintenance Phase to come alongside those currently in Track 1 and help them with any struggles that they may be having. The mentors will be chosen from the Therapists and Therapy Team here at FSP and will be made available to them if needed to create an environment of learning and understanding in instances where there are gaps in the sections. mentors will also be utilizing their **skills in the program by staying involved in** group sessions when/if needed while also staying involved in any new treatment objectives that will help further their education/experience while preparing to leave prison and reintegrate back into society.

## Objective

To utilize the experience that many of our Track 1 clients have gained through this program here at FSP and allow them a chance to help those still in group to better recognize their risks, protective factors, and overall understanding of the material. The goal of SOTMP is to never again create another victim, and our goal comes alongside that and asks that we help keep each other accountable throughout group and the learning process. One of the aspects that this program will meet, that has never been addressed, is when group is not in session, the clients are still surrounded by one another the rest of the day/week, without having the ability to be in contact with their therapist for issues and questions. Now this program will not replace the therapists obviously, nor will a mentor be another therapist, they will just be available to help in times where there are questions, concerns or conflicts and therapists are not available to help. The main objective will be to use their experience to illustrate how to successfully deal with group and the stressors, anxieties and difficulties that come with it, while being able to lead by example how to manage risks and live life in a healthy manner utilizing the tools that have been learned through Track 1 of SOTMP.

## Benefits

The benefits are unlimited as it now provides for more help in areas where therapists are not able to help at. There are 168 hours in the week, and clients in the program are in group only 3 hours out of that time, which leaves 165 hours where there is a real need to help in dealing with situations that arise. Throughout any given day there are conflicts that happen in the pod, the day-hall, the chow-hall, recreation, library, and this is just to name a few. This is the day-to-day issues that best simulate what life in the community will be like, and it is the area that is least impacted by a therapist and support. A mentor will be able to empathize in these situations, as they have unquestionably been through something similar. But they can also work through the problem in a healthy way, while giving support and encouragement to all involved. The goal of the mentor is not to give the answers or solve all problems that may arise, but it is to demonstrate skills and knowledge of how to handle a situation rationally and diffuse potential altercations or issues that could become something worse prior to a one-on-one appointment of a group meeting.

\*\*\*

What you just read was my proposal that addressed all their requests as well as proactively looking ahead to what their "nos" would be from a DOC and administrative point of view. Knowing through my experience of creating several things inside of the Department of Corrections, I went ahead and created the criteria that must be met to apply to be a mentor as well as the application process, including a questionnaire that takes the burden off the therapist. I then presented the program to the therapists and administration. A few weeks later, it was signed off on. Mentor program created and implemented. Thank God.

God doesn't waste a thing.

# 54

Now I am not an expert on the miracles of the Bible, how to rank them by level of difficulty or which one or the other is/was more impactful. That is for others much smarter than me to debate. I wish I could put into words the miraculous things I have experienced God do. Well, I guess, in a way, that is what this book is. What I am trying to emphasize is the miraculous doorway God opened for myself and a friend of mine, who was also in the mentor program I had just created, to walk through. I can only compare it to God parting the DOC "sea" to save a group of people often forgotten and rarely fought for—the men in the Sex Offender Treatment Program. But more than that, the ones on the century-long waitlist.

My friend Isaac served sixteen years before he got into SOTMP and was instrumental in this miracle taking place. One day, after he and I were finished working out on the yard, we began to chat about how many things in the curriculum were confusing, missing, in the wrong order, or just plain wrong. A few moments later, we had paper out and a workbook that DOC provided for us, and we began to dissect it and make notes about if we could fix it and how we would do it. By the end of the night, Isaac and I had completely reorganized the order in which the content should be taught, to best build on prior knowledge and lessons, so the men in SOTMP would better understand their treatment. He and I did not begin to touch the actual material of the workbook, just the order of it at this point. This is our "build the ark" moment as we had a feeling a flood was coming. I just had to go looking for the rain.

I went to work at the furniture shop, professionally typed up the outline of what we felt should be taught and in what order, with explanations of why this was best. Not only did we create the outline, but we also documented which assignments would be used to demonstrate understanding. We also created ideas of new assignments that would be beneficial. We added in talking points about how to progress clients through the program to get more men through with less stress on the therapists. Once this was all done and typed, it was time to step out in faith.

I walked into my next session with Mr. G and told him I had something I would like to chat with him about, separate from the mentor program we just created. He asked what it was, and I began with, "All due respect, Mr. G, but the curriculum that you are using here is unorganized and, honestly, more detrimental than it is helpful in many regards. It is confusing for most to follow and often leads to more questions than answers. But don't worry, I got the solution for you."

It was at this point that I had his complete attention because I was about to present to him a solution for a problem he and the DOC didn't even know they had. After walking him through the outline to show that nothing required, as far as content and regulations that must be met, for the California Sex Offender Management Board was removed, so we could all stay within state standards and guidelines, he asked two questions and made one statement. His question was, "How in the world were you able to organize this, and what in the world makes you believe that you are qualified to do this?"

Both questions garnered the same response of "Back in 2007, I got a master's degree in curriculum and instruction that I never used as a math teacher."

This was followed up with his statement of "Go ahead and create the new curriculum, and then we can present it to DOC administration for their overall approval."

I asked him for a few things, including the therapists' schedules, as we were going to implement an entire new way of teaching, learning, progressing, and graduating through the program. He gave it to me, and off I went.

For the next eight workdays at the furniture shop, Isaac and I sat together, with the permission and support of our boss, the major, and we completely overhauled the entire SOTMP curriculum. It was truly amazing. We sat in an office working around six other men, who normally would have been upset we were getting paid the same amount as them but not actually doing a thing to help the shop out for those days. All of them in the office with us knew we were creating this to help others, and as it turned out, five of them would eventually need to take the program to leave DOC, so they were thankful for the effort and change.

In less than two weeks, the project was completed, and we were asked to teach the therapists how to utilize the curriculum to get maximum results and help the most men out of each class, month, and year. This teaching was exciting as just two months prior, I was sitting in a group learning from many of these same therapists, and now I've been placed in a position to teach them and make their lives easier. Most of the therapists were accepting as they saw the benefits of the new curriculum and the way it was organized. However, several were not thrilled as my teaching was met with trepidation on their parts. Their behavior was fine; it didn't offend me. I realized it was more a challenge to their self-esteem and ego than it was mine. I clearly saw how God was working in this situation, and it further proved God would use anything, from anytime in a life, to accomplish His goals. I was a math teacher for seven years and never once thought of using my master's to write new curriculum while teaching, but God had me get that degree for a different reason. The curriculum was approved and adopted by DOC.

God doesn't waste a thing.

# 55

After it was used for a while, Isaac and I noticed the fruit of the work put in as more people began to understand their treatment and ultimately graduate the course. This led to more people getting paroled and returning home to their families. There is nothing as thrilling and emotional as seeing someone get told they will be released tomorrow, so pack up your property and be ready by 4:15 in the morning. That moment brings feelings of excitement, nervousness, sadness, and about a thousand others words don't do justice. Bringing families together, restoring freedom, creating opportunities for reconciliation are all biblical principles, and watching many men walk into that was awesome. Knowing I had a hand in it, well, that was heartwarming.

I got told by Mr. G I had been accepted into a halfway house and that I was going to be leaving soon. The date I was given was May 27, 2020. When I was told this date, I was overwhelmed. I cried, and I hit my knees. I thanked God. I called and thanked my parents. I thanked everyone who had poured into my life for as long as they had.

There are several moments I must share because I believe God doesn't waste a thing, and these memories will forever be with me. They may just be the most polarizing moments of my last few years as they were raw, unplanned, and a direct representation of what God's love looks and feels like. The story of how I learned I was getting released is one of them.

I was at work when my boss, the major, and Mr. G called me into the office and had me shut the door. My boss stood up and gave me a hug, telling me he was proud of me and that I would be leaving prison soon. I had gotten accepted to leave, and I realized what that meant. I would be able to go and see my grandmother's grave. I could play golf my with dad. I will be able to go on drives with my mom. I could hang out with my brother, sister-in-law, and see my nephews while they were still in high school. I literally could not shut off my brain.

As I wiped off the tears and got up to leave his office, my heart knew immediately where to go. I walked out to shipping, where Ethan, Sammy, and Brenton all were, as Mr. G followed. I made a beeline for Ethan. I grabbed his shoulder. He turned and must have seen my eyes were red because before I could even say a word, he put his work down and buried my head into his shoulder, and he just hugged me. I managed to whisper to him, "Ethan, I get to go home," and he began to cry with me and tell me how happy he was for me.

I must have just stood there for five minutes, crying and hugging him. I also hugged Brenton and Sammy. They were excited as well, but it was different with Ethan. See, what is unique about Ethan is he might be the most caring and loving person I met throughout my time in DOC, and he is serving a sentence where most would get jealous, angry, or depressed when others get good news. Not him. He gets filled with joy and shares it. It's a gift and one I honestly don't think I could possess. It is one of the many reasons I continually prayed for him as I didn't want the time that I was with him in prison to be the last that I see him.

For the next few weeks, I began to make my calls to friends on the streets and tell them the good news and that God had once again worked in the impossible and delivered me from a twenty-year sentence over a decade early. I also made my rounds to thank the staff members who encouraged me to keep pushing forward and hoping for a great future. Then the date came up, and I was down to less than two weeks.

God doesn't waste a thing.

# 56

This brings me to the second of the several moments that will forever stick out in my heart. As I knew I would be leaving early on the twenty-seventh, I wanted to spend the last night hanging out with my best buds. I got permission from Sergeant Stenson, the same one who helped me get acquainted with FSP three years prior, to get Sammy, Ethan, James, and Brenton all out on the yard the night of the twenty-sixth to just walk, talk, and sit on the bleachers. I knew this night would be tough, and I didn't know how I was going to feel about it or certainly handle it. I had started telling them and others how I felt about them long ago as I didn't want to miss that chance like I did at SQSP. I wrote an article about saying goodbye to them in the newspaper, and I wrote personal letters to them as well, but I still was not prepared to say bye that evening.

At 7:30 that night, my new reality was setting in, I knew I had only about an hour left with these guys, and as weird as it sounds, I didn't want the night to end. I didn't want them to call movement to bring the yard in. On one hand, I wanted to go home. Of course, I wanted to leave prison, yet on the other hand, that meant the possibility of never again seeing or talking to my friends, truly an emotional battle, which I knew I had to give to God and trust that He will restore our communication and relationships on His time. As usual, God worked it out in a way that far exceeded my expectations. I was allowed to be placed on all their phone lists as well as being the first guy on parole to be placed on a permanent visiting list while on parole, back at a facility I just left, to see Ethan once a month. Praise God.

Anyways, back to my last night—as we were all heading up the ramp to enter back into the facility, I began to feel the tears welling up in my eyes as I was fully aware of the next one hundred yards. I got to my unit, which was the first stop in the hallway, and I continued to chat with Sammy, James, Brenton, and Ethan, who all lived in unit 8, which is another one hundred yards down the hall. Eventually, there was nobody in the hallway but the four of us and Sergeant Stenson, who stood at a distance, fully aware of what was going on. I hugged Sammy, James, and Brenton and told them I loved them and I would see them soon as they were all eligible for release around 2023, then I turned to Ethan. This was different. This hurt. As Ethan and I cried, I knew this could potentially be the last time I ever see him. I couldn't let go. I couldn't say bye. He taught me to love unconditionally while showing me that I am capable of walking tall and strong, believing in myself during scary moments. I couldn't turn and walk away from him. It was now ten minutes past them ending movement, and he and I stood there in the hallway. Eventually, Sergeant Stenson had to step in and nudge Ethan along, and I am so thankful it was Stenson who was there, that was a total God moment, as he had allowed us to have that moment. I walked up the steps, called my parents for the last time ever from inside of a prison, went to room B11, where I hung out with my friend and brother Hadley, until the morning came, and I was asked to leave prison.

God doesn't waste a thing.

# 57

I spent nearly seven years in prison, seven years for my own selfish, harmful actions; seven years away from my family, my friends, my freedoms, and in a large part, my future. Or so I thought. Let me make this point perfectly clear: I do not want to serve one more day inside the Department of Corrections as an inmate. However, I do not regret any of those days because it created the man I am today. Those blessings and miracles I was fortunate to walk through formed in me a passion for God and all His children. God was with me the whole time, and even though I wasn't with my biological family inside, God placed around me brothers in Christ, deep friendships, and thousands of the most joy-filled moments of my life. Those seven years inside, I am grateful for them. It molded me into the best son, brother, uncle, citizen, friend, employee, and follower of Christ I could be. I am thankful God has blessed me with the ability to see His love and faithfulness in a way that allows me to share it with others. Everything worked out how it was supposed to. All things do work together for good, and God can use anything to bring about His will for your life as well.

God doesn't waste a thing.

# EPILOGUE

Having the beauty of hindsight and the ability to look back on all these amazing miracles as a Christ follower, I can point to numerous moments that have forever changed my life and how I perceive Jesus and His unending love for me. But one stands above the rest. The event that sent this entire story in motion, the catalyst if you will, was the night I called my best friend Nate, my brother Lee, and my parents on the phone to tell them I loved them, that I had made a choice where the consequence of my action is going to be beyond my ability to cope, and I was going to go lay on a train track and end my life. It is important to note, at this time, I was in San Francisco, and everyone I called was about five hours away, if not more. I made the calls then turned my phone off and found the track. I lay down, saw the lights in the distance, and felt the tracks rumble as the train drew closer. I closed my eyes and awaited the end.

When I stood up from that track, after being blessed that the train went by behind me on another one of the tracks at this location, I would have never thought this was the setup for the greatest example of Jesus and His actions of love for His kids. When I got back to my car, which I had hidden in a crowded parking lot, a parking lot I later came to realize was the parking lot to WSP, I still felt scared that the police were out looking for me, so I drove around San Francisco for about four hours, until I was nearing the end of an emptying gas tank. I decided, at this point, to head home, and after parking my car and scanning the area for police officers, I headed up the stairs to my place on the third floor. I opened the door and stepped inside and looked to the left, down the hallway of my place, and saw my father standing there with his arms stretched out in front of him. I looked at him and could see the tears in his eyes as he was clearly crying from the thought of me being dead. I watched as those tears of panic switched to tears of joy as he saw that I was alive. I asked him, "What are you doing here?"

To which he replied, "I didn't know what else to do when you hung up."

I looked at him and again pointed out, "Dad, my plan was to kill myself on the tracks. What were you planning on doing when you got here?"

It was at this point he uttered words that will forever be implanted in my head and on my heart. "I promised your mother and God, when you and your brother were born, that I would take care of you guys until the day I died, so I came."

My father had no reason to think I was going to come home, he had no reason to believe I would still be alive, but his actions were not dictated by my decision. His love for me was not predicated by what I had done. He ran to me. He met me in my worst of times, right where I was at. He greeted me with open arms and without judgment or yelling. My dad did not yell at me for what I did or blame me for the phone call I made that night. He never called me names or made me feel worse for an action I took, one that I was fully aware was wrong while committing my crime that created a victim. He didn't tell me I needed to do a list of things before he would grab me and hug me. He did none of that, ever. He came. I called; he came. The way my father treated me during this time and how he responded to this event is the most real example of our Heavenly Father I have ever seen, read about, or experienced in my life. It is what I call the "Prodigal Father" moment. In the Bible, they have the story of the "Prodigal Son" coming home to his father. Well, my father came to me. This is one of many reasons why my father is my hero. He is, other than Jesus, the most important, inspirational, and loving person in my life, period. I am so grateful I got to learn what it means to act like Jesus and to love like Jesus by watching my father through, not just in this situation, but in the next decade worth of events as well. My dad and mom stayed with me and supported me through all the moments you just finished reading about as well as the thousands of other moments that couldn't fit in this book.

Please don't misunderstand what I am saying. My father is not Jesus.

He merely just figured out how to respond like Jesus, which is in love. The best part of this realization is that our Father in heaven is infinitely more loving than my dad. Our Father in heaven is more present, intelligent, available, and embracing than any of our own fathers, mothers, brothers, sisters, or friends will ever be. I want to encourage all of you to know that our Heavenly Father is standing there with His arms wide open right now, waiting for you to come. All you need to do is go to Him. I stared at my dad in that hallway for what seemed to be like an hour but was more like two minutes before I did just that. I went to him and felt his arms wrap around me. You have a Heavenly Father who loves you, who wants a relationship with you, who wants to embrace you. God has already come to you, His arms are already open, and He's already said, "Come." All you need to do now is go to Him.

CPSIA information can be obtained
at www.ICGtesting.com
Printed in the USA
JSHW010807050223
37278JS00002B/10